Science Is Simple

By Peggy Ashbrook

Illustrations: Marie Ferrante-Doyle

Dedication

To my parents who, as my first teachers, set me on
    this path
To Helen O'Hear, my kindergarten teacher, who
    saw my future
To the children, parents, and staff of Valley Drive
    Cooperative Preschool, "Thank you for doing
    science with me"
And to Darryl, for his encouragement and
    confidence in me

Note from the Author

Gentle Readers,
Please write to me. I am interested in hearing your
thoughts on teaching science to young children,
on this book, and on activities in it. You may
contact me at scienceissimple@yahoo.com or
through Gryphon House, Inc. at 10726 Tucker
Street, Beltsville MD 20705. Thank you for doing
science with young children.

—Peggy Ashbrook

Acknowledgments

With grateful thanks to the City of Alexandria
librarians, especially Linda Sinclair and Lisa
Springer, for much help finding books relating to
science concepts; to my father-in-law, Pedrito
François, for the computer that prompted me to
start writing; to Kathy Charner, my editor, for her
hard work and hand-holding to make the work of
this novice into a book and for her wonderful
idea to include letters home to parents for each
lesson; and to all the preschool teachers who
welcomed me into their classrooms.

Science Is Simple

Over 250 Activities for Preschoolers

Peggy Ashbrook
Illustrations: Marie Ferrante-Doyle

gryphon house, inc.
Beltsville, Maryland

Copyright

Library of Congress Cataloging-in-Publication Data

Ashbrook, Peggy.
  Science is simple / by Peggy Ashbrook ;
illustrations, Marie Ferrante-Doyle.
    p. cm.
Includes bibliographical references and index.
  ISBN 978-0-87659-272-4
  1. Science--Study and teaching (Early childhood)-
-Activity programs. I. Title.
  LB1139.5.S35A84 2003
  372.3'5--dc21
              2002155622

Bulk purchase

Disclaimer

Table of Contents

Bubbles

Objective 203

Science Table 203

To Get Ready—Exploring Bubbles 204

Feel Air 204

Blow Air Into Water to Make Bubbles 204

What Is the Shape of a Bubble? 204

Can You Make a Square Bubble? 205

Books to Read 205

Follow-Up Activity .205

Bringing Science Home! A Note Home to
     Families About Bubbles 206

Recycling Paper to Use Again

Objective 207

Science Table 207

To Get Ready 207

Feel Many Kinds of Paper 207

What Does It Mean to Re-Use Something? . .208

What Does It Mean to Recycle Something? . .208

Prepare for Recycling Paper 209

Change the Shape of Newspaper 209

Recycled Paper, Step 1 210

Recycled Paper, Step 2 210

Making Papier-Mâché From Newspapers .211

The Resources of the Earth Are Precious . .212

Books to Read 212

Website to Visit 212

Bringing Science Home! A Note Home to
     Families About Recycling Paper 213

Rocket Ships Blasting Off

Objectives 214

Science Table 214

To Get Ready—Exploring Rocket Ships . . .214

How Do Rockets Work? 215

The Power of Gas .216

Fuel for the Pretend Rocket 216

Blast Off! 216

Books to Read 217

Website to Visit 217

Follow-Up Activities 217

Bringing Science Home! A Note Home to
     Families About Rocket Ships Blasting
     Off 218

Making Solutions

Objective 219

Science Table 219

To Get Ready—Exploring Solutions 219

Identifying Plain Water 219

Identify the Solids .220

Mix the Liquid and the Solids 220

Comparing the Results 221

Taste the Water to Find the Sugar 221

Follow-Up Activities 222

Bringing Science Home! A Note Home to
     Families About Making Solutions 223

Measuring Hands

Objective 224

Science Table 224

To Get Ready—Exploring Measuring 224

Make a Set of Measuring Hands 224

Measure With a Hand 225

Measure With Many Hands 226

Books to Read 226

Follow-Up Activities 226

Bringing Science Home! A Note Home to
     Families About Measuring Hands 227

Writing Additional Lessons **228**

Appendix

Resources 232

Complete Book List 233

Out-of-Print (But Recommended)
     Book List 240

Index **243**

Introduction

Like learning to count or to read, learning how to "do" science is a lifelong process. Children of all ages benefit from exposure to "science" situations. They need to be encouraged to experience the world fully, describe what they see, ask questions about it, repeat the experience, and think about the why of it.

By not doing science from the beginning we give our children the idea that it is too hard to attempt. If we want our children to perform well when they are in high school, we need to include science in their early childhood curriculum.

Exposing the children to pre-experimental activities such as collecting rocks, bouncing balls, reading about dinosaurs and cooking (all science activities), giving them the vocabulary to discuss their ideas, and creating opportunities for them to ask questions and seek answers— all fit into any early childhood curriculum.

It is quite different to learn about something rather than to experience it. Both kinds of these learning activities are appropriate. For example, dinosaurs fascinate many preschoolers; however, it is impossible to experience these creatures firsthand. Yet, fossils of all kinds can be the subject and the basis for a hands-on experience.

Science Happens Every Day

Many everyday activities offer opportunities to focus on a science concept. Pouring juice is a chance to comment on how the fluid always goes down. Noticing that there is a difference between working with dry sand and wet sand, that water spilled on our clothes evaporates, that leaves move in the wind, that a ball rolls down a slope— all of these ordinary occurrences are opportunities to ask questions to focus children's attention on *why* it happens the way it does.

Listen to these preschoolers as they look at and hold roly-poly bugs and slugs. In this everyday experience—looking at bugs outside—they are making observations, classifying, using tools, making hypotheses, counting, describing, and drawing conclusions. In other words, they are doing the work of scientists.

Will	*I see something there.*
Natalia	*Can I hold it? Can I touch it?*
Heather	*I was making it bigger. (Using a magnifier.)*
Miguel	*Look, there's two animals.*
Simran	*It's on your finger!*
Maya	*I like the roly-poly.*
Eric	*Hey, look, there's another one!*
Rhea	*It's just resting.*
Sarin	*It's tickling you, Ja-mante, and it tickled me.*
Rose	*This slug is longer.*
Braxton	*Where is it? Right there! Under the leaf.*
Todd	*I'm a slug. (And he slides all the way back to the classroom.)*
Brooke	*This is what you usually do when you don't want your pet to fall. (As the roly-poly moves from hand to hand.)*

Amila   *This one can turn like a ball. (A roly-poly.)*
Joey   *These are yucky, gooey bugs. I'm being nice to them.*
Josua   *They're looking for something to eat.*

Focus on and repeat everyday experiences, such as working with simple machines. Is there a child who practically empties the liquid soap container every time she washes her hands? Fascinated by the feel of the soap or wondering how the pump works, this child needs to repeat the experience to work it out to her own satisfaction. Fill the container with colored water and let her pump until she's satisfied.

If a child can learn, as even three-year-olds do, to distinguish between and pronounce the names of the dinosaurs, such as Brachiosaurus and Tyrannosaurus, then they can learn the words *solution, ovipositor, reflect, vibration,* and *hypothesis.* Use scientific words when appropriate, and be consistent in your use.

What If You Don't Have an Interest or Background in Science?

The lessons in this book lead both children and teachers to observe everyday happenings in a focused setting. Just as you do not need to be a fire marshal to draw children's attention to a passing fire truck, or a doctor to talk with the children about a recent illness, you do not need to know all the answers before teaching about what you see happening in the world.

Common, everyday experiences, such as watching a bird take flight or blowing bubbles, are the basis for the science experiences in this book. It is your willingness to draw the children's attention to these happenings that is important, not your knowledge or training in science. You do need to be a resource and be willing to model how to look for answers that you do not know. Other teachers and parents are good resources, as are many wonderful science books in the children's section of your local public library. These books explain scientific concepts in age-appropriate language.

Keep this book nearby during the lesson. It will remind you to ask certain questions that the children may not raise. And it will help you remember that most of what happens in science should be the children's job. The teacher's job is to do the groundwork so that the "dominoes" will fall into place as the children do the activity.

When Children Have Questions

Most of the "science moments" you experience with children won't be the only time children will have that experience. They will have other opportunities to build on their knowledge and perhaps come to the same conclusion that an adult does. When a child asks a question, it's best to return the question to them by asking, "What do you think?" After making time for the child to answer the question, you can be a resource for them, as needed.

In addition, encourage children to question everyday experiences. For example, a child might say, "Look at this footprint in the mud! It's probably a bear." Although you know this is unlikely (unless you live in bear country), encourage the child to question, wonder, and guess about this "science moment." Ask some leading questions such as, "How big are bears?" "Where do bears live?" or "What other animals live around here?" before (if you ever do) telling the child, "No, that's a dog's footprint."

What If They Ask a Question I Can't Answer?

Encouraging children to ask questions means that sooner or later one will ask a question you can't answer, at least without doing some research. Telling a child, "I don't know. How do you think we could find out?" will show him not only how he can find answers, but also that it's okay to say, "I don't know." Ask other people and, of course, use the library, which has introductory science books that will provide some answers.

What Size Group Works Best?

It is hard for young children to take turns making observations, asking questions, and sharing their experiences. The challenge is to set up the experience so that every child will have a chance to question, wonder, and guess.

A group size that works for one group, one school, or one teacher may not work for another. Consider the interests and abilities of the children you teach. One or more of the following techniques may work for your group when science is a choice during free play time:

- Try science activities that have no beginning and no end, so children can participate for a few minutes, leave the activity and become involved with something else, but then return to the science activity a few minutes later. (An example of this kind of activity is Magnets and Testing Hypotheses, page 27 or Compost Critters, page 59.)
- Repeat science activities periodically.
- Prepare materials ahead of time and put them on a shelf or in a lidded box, ready to take out when time or interest allows.
- Allow time for extended science activities, as some children will work longer with the materials if they have a particular interest in the subject matter.

Small Groups

If you are able to do science activities with a small group, gather at a table or around a "science circle"—a round tablecloth spread on the floor in an out-of-the-way corner. Explain to the other children that they will have a turn, and it will be more fun for them to share with fewer children, making this tough job of waiting a little easier. If you are able to take the small group to another room, it will allow for uninterrupted focus on the experience and preserve the element of surprise. Not knowing the ending in some lessons can increase the opportunities for every child to hypothesize about what they think will happen. It can also be more fun to have a surprise ending.

Doing science during small-group time is another way to make sure science remains a hands-on experience for all the children. If you have enough materials, all small groups can participate at the same time. And, while the children are having their outdoor time, you can take a small group aside to do one of the outdoor experiences, such as any of the planting experiences, Bubbles (page 203), or Wheels Are Tools (page 198).

At the end of our small-group science time, I use a ritual to signal that science time is over and they have to relinquish the materials. As a group we say the following poem:

All Join In
by Avelyn Davidson
As wide as a gate, (arms and legs stretched out wide)
As tall as a house, (stand tall with arms reaching up)
As thin as a pin, (arms held straight at your sides)

As small as a mouse, (crouch down and
squeak)
As bent as a branch, (bend your arms)
As round as a ball, (curve arms with hands
touching)
Now stand up straight as that is all. (stand
straight and open arms out)
*(Permission granted from Shortland Publications 2B
Cawley, St. Ellerslie Auckland, New Zealand)*

If you are not able to "do" science in small groups, simply break the science lesson down to its parts—the activities. Introduce one or two activities a day over the course of the week to allow all the children time for each part of the experience.

Self-Selected or Teacher-Chosen Groups

It's wonderful to be able to immediately satisfy a child's curiosity and desire to work. Allowing children to self-select to participate in a science activity encourages their interest. But sometimes when you bring out the materials for a new science activity, all the children want to be first. That is when you must choose groups rather than doing science with the children who are first interested, especially if you have limited materials or space.

If you select science groups, try to teach the active children together—the ones who call out their observations first, who bump and jostle, who grab from their neighbors and have no problem telling their neighbors to give it back. They thrive in a group where they don't have to wait for a quieter child to speak or finish using the materials. The quieter children benefit from doing science with children who also wait for someone else to speak first, speak more slowly, or wait to be given permission before doing anything. This gives them the opportunity to be the initiators.

The Scientific Method

Using the scientific method, like using your manners, can become a habit at an early age. For preschoolers, this means encouraging a questioning sense, a desire to find answers, and an ability to come up with a question.

Following the scientific method means focusing attention on what you think will happen, making a prediction even if, for preschoolers, it is a guess. You can help children learn to do this any time you read to them, by asking them to predict what will happen next in the story. Ask children often, "What do you think will happen next?"

In *Creepy Crawlies and the Scientific Method,* Sally Kneidel describes how an activity differs from an experiment:

> *"An activity is simply watching something, or perhaps interacting with it in some way so as to cause a reaction. For example, feeding a live cricket to a praying mantis is an activity. Many people call activities experiments. But an experiment is an activity that is designed to answer a question and has a control to rule out other interpretations of the result. An experiment is more valuable to a child's learning because it encourages more thinking."*

> *(Reprinted with permission of publisher © 1993. Fulcrum Publishing, Inc. Golden Colorado. All rights reserved.)*

Although this level of scientific inquiry, an experiment, is developmentally beyond most preschoolers, they can learn the ideas of hypothesis, procedure, results, and conclusion. When a child formulates a hypothesis, it makes the *science experience* the child's own. Children should get a chance to say what they think will happen before an activity begins and certainly before an adult speaks. Do not let your eagerness to share phenomena spoil the outcome.

The Scientific Method raises these questions:
  *Whose job is it to answer them?

	Question	**Who Should Answer**
Purpose:	Why are you doing this experiment?	The teacher
Hypothesis:	What do you think will happen?	The children
Procedure:	How will you test your hypothesis?	The children and the teacher
Materials:	What did you use to do the experiment?	The teacher's job is to provide the materials
Results:	What happened?	The children
Conclusion:	Why do you think that happened?	The children

Once you present the activity, keep quiet and allow the children time to come up with a hypothesis, a statement about what *they* think it is or what *they* think will happen. It is your job to wait for children to formulate their ideas. It will become a habit, the more you practice. If the children find a bug on the playground and they ask you, "What is it?" say, "What do you think it is? What is it doing? Where did you find it, on the ground, on a bush?" Encourage them to recognize or build their store of knowledge about the bug.

At times children will want you to act as a source of information for them. When this is clearly what they are looking for, answer the question or help them find the answer in a book.

Science Is Not Magic

An important part of the scientific method is repeating the experiment with the same result. Can another child get the same results? When we experiment with mixing and separating colors, I wait for one child to discover that putting the blue and yellow acetate circles together makes green. Another child may remark, "Hey! Mine does too! Does yours, Saheed? Does yours, Vanessa?" Children learn that science is not magic when they make it happen and can repeat it over and

over. The result *they* get is not because you have special powers or because you said a magic word, it's because of the nature of the materials. It happens every time you do the same thing. Point out this repetition of results to them during the science experience because they may be so busy with the materials that they may not notice what others are doing.

Be Flexible About What Is Being Taught

Part of the excitement in teaching science to young children is that they often follow their own urges to manipulate the materials and may not imitate the modeled behavior. For example, in making cardboard tube "kazoos," some children will discover that if they blow, instead of humming, the wax paper covering the end will fly off. It may take a few minutes for everyone to try it, dissolve into giggles, and test to see who can send theirs the farthest. This may disrupt the teaching of Sound Is Vibration (page 164), but it's great fun and great science (they are discovering their world!). We want children to notice what is happening; not to sit still and listen to what other people say is happening. That's why the kazoo-making is best at the end of the Sound Is

Vibration lesson. Eventually, everyone wants to achieve both the flying wax paper and the vibrating noise generated by humming. Incorporate children's discoveries into the experience or introduce the materials ahead of time so they have time to get their "sillies" out.

How Much Should I Push the Children to Be Adventurous?

It always amazes me when a child wants to taste a tiny pinch of sand. Part of Making Solutions (page 219) is to look at, feel, and taste water, sugar, and sand to find out what it is, not what we think it is. Remind children that it's safe to use our senses this way because the teacher has planned the lesson and knows what the substances are and that they are safe. Surprisingly, many of the children want to taste the sand and surprisingly, some of them don't want to taste the sugar, even after other children ask for more. Always taste first and then ask, "Who wants to taste the white solid?" Expect many to shout "ME!" Offer every child a taste, but don't try to talk her into it. Respect their cautious approach.

On the other hand, observation should not be the only skill they practice in science activities. Hands-on science engages the senses, a powerful memory tool. A child who consistently won't handle anything on a tray of objects picked for their range of textures can be brought to touch most of them by being given a task. Hand the child the most common, dry, smooth object and instruct him to "Please put this in the box for me." That gives him a way to handle the object for a defined and brief amount of time. Usually the child goes on to touch the other objects. With things that might be "icky," ask all the children to "get one finger ready to touch" so even the most adventurous/least discriminating initially use one finger. It seems that a one-finger touch is a reasonably safe approach and serves to get the cautious child started and out of the watching mode.

Extending the Experience

Will children think about the science activity again in five minutes or remember it later? Yes, especially if you provide the opportunity. By reading one of the large number of children's books that contain a science theme in the story, you encourage children to think again about the science lesson, whether it's about a seed growing, water moving, the way rocks feel in the hand, or what an insect was doing. Extend the experience again on the playground when you point out a similar experience. Each science lesson has suggestions for activities to do ahead and activities to do as a follow-up. The Science Table (or Cart or Basket) is the place to put durable materials related to the experience. Rotate them! Some tools, such as magnifying glasses, should always be available, but don't keep a fossil or the tornado tube bottle out all the time or it quickly loses appeal and thus its ability to teach.

What Materials Are Needed?

The key resource is books, books, and more books: children's literature, non-fiction books on the topic (also helpful as resources for teachers on background information), books on teaching science to young children, and books of experiences/experiments to get additional ideas. Books are the bedrock of your science program.

Found materials, or the throwaways of our culture, are the second most important component. Recycle containers of all kinds, and materials such as cardboard, foam, and fabric into your science equipment. An oversized plastic jar that held pretzels can be converted into an insect habitat. Mylar plastic bags used to package snack foods are mirrored on the inside. Once emptied, washed and dried, they make flexible mirrors or rockets.

To do the activities in this book, you will have to purchase very few specialized materials. The purchased materials mentioned in the book usually come from party stores, craft stores, school supply stores, and school science supply companies, some of which are listed in the Appendix on page 232.

How to Use This Book

For each lesson, there are directions for the teacher and suggested questions, both of which are designed to guide the children's actions to discovery. Do not make those discoveries for them!

Begin with one lesson. As you gather the materials, think of it as building a library of science materials. The found and recycled materials you gather can be stored for the next year as a kit, each year adding several kits.

The science concepts presented in the activities crop up again and again throughout the year. Think of teaching science as an on-going process; you are never really finished with a topic. You can cover it many times in many ways in varying depth. Sometimes you plan a topic and sometimes the children suggest it. Each science lesson in *Science Is Simple* has the following sections:

- Objective(s)
- Science Table
- To Get Ready
- Activities (Materials, What to Do, What to Talk About)
- Follow-Up Activities
- Books to Read
- Bringing Science Home

The objective states what you want the child to accomplish and discover during the activity. The objects on the Science Table give children independent, repeated opportunities to understand the concepts. Contributed objects such as special stones or seeds should be available for examination for a few weeks before being retired to their collection box or sent home. Keeping the materials in the classroom for several weeks provides time for additional child-directed discovery.

The activities, if done in sequence, build on each other. Each activity includes:

- Materials
- To Get Ready
- What to Do
- What to Talk About

A day or a week before you want to begin the science lesson, do the "To Get Ready" section, which introduces the topic or concept. Initiating a conversation about insects, for example, gives the children plenty of time to tell their own insect stories before experiencing Crickets and Using Magnifiers (page 55).

The "What to Do" and "What to Talk About" sections for each activity give step-by-step instructions and open-ended questions to lead the children to discovery. You and the children may discover the information (which is in parentheses), or you may decide to tell it to them. To help children begin to answer their own questions about what is going on, frequently ask them to describe what they are experiencing.

Follow-up activities present the same concepts in a different way, often with materials that the children can handle independently. For example, keeping a terrarium of crickets in the classroom will give the children many more chances to continue observing insects. A Science Table is the perfect place to put the materials for the follow-up activities and to leave them out for a few weeks. Children may gloss over familiar objects so, unless you intend to make the crickets the classroom pets, rotate them out and let the Science Table objects from the next lesson take their place.

Reading the suggested books, or just having them available for the children's use, gives the children a chance to casually notice facts about the topic or see the concept in the context of everyday life. Body parts unique to insects are much more easily identified when the children have pored over the photographs in an insect identification book before seeing the live insect. This careful groundwork sets the stage for more focused attention during the lesson and integrates the activities into the day instead of it being an isolated activity.

"Bringing Science Home" offers letters to families to inform them about what their children have been doing in the classroom and to invite their participation.

Children want to handle everything themselves, and they enjoy repeating the activities. When possible, provide one of everything for each child. Keep in mind that the goal is to have the children make observations, gain information, and come to conclusions through their use of the materials. It may take longer than just one activity, one lesson, or one day.

Think of each science lesson as a recipe—a recipe in progress, because every time the children do the activities, they will teach you new ways of presenting and using the material, and new questions to ask and seek to answer.

Getting Started—The First Lessons

A good place to begin is the lesson on children's literature to teach the scientific method (pages 24-26). This will give you practice asking (but not answering) the children's questions, and give them practice answering them. Other experiences that introduce the tools of scientists are Measuring Hands (pages 224-227), Crickets and Using Magnifiers (pages 55-58), What Is It? (pages 122-125), and Magnets and Testing Hypotheses (pages 27-32). For young preschoolers, the experiences about our senses are a good way to draw them into science. Mixing and Separating Colors (pages 190-193), Sound Is Vibration (pages 164-168), Our Sense of Smell (pages 194-197), and Our Sense of Touch (pages 186-189) involve activities that take about five minutes but can last for 30 or more minutes as some children repeat the activity over and over and some children just drop by for a few minutes.

Or, begin with a topic that is your favorite or one that reflects the children's current interests. Of course, try the activity before you do it with the children. Try it with your co-teachers and all of you will be one step ahead. Many of the science lessons can become science kits if you store the materials together. On the outside of the box, inventory the materials in the box and list those you must gather new each year.

Science Is Simple
A Year of Experiences

Please note that the suggested time and location for presenting the experience are based on the weather in the Washington, DC area, agricultural zone 7.
The seasons may occur earlier or later where you live.

Suggested season for doing the experience	Title of the experience
first quarter	Using children's literature to teach the scientific method
first quarter	Magnets and testing hypotheses
early Fall	Year-round gardening
early Fall	Planting strawberry plants
early Fall	What do seeds need to grow?
Fall	Why do some tree leaves change color?
Fall, outside	Stretch your senses on a walk to a nearby park
Fall, before the frost	Crickets and using magnifiers
Fall, before the frost	Compost critters
Fall, before the end of October	Planting spring bulbs
Fall	Corn and an introduction to the globe
Winter	Winter birds
Winter	What is melting?
Spring	What can the wind do?
February, outside	Planting peas on Presidents' Day
by April 15	Waiting for mantises to hatch
Spring	A tree is nice
Spring, outside	Dirt, what is it?
by May 1	Butterflies change as they grow
late Spring, outside	Planting a butterfly garden

Additional Lessons for Any Time of Year

Title of the experience

What is it?
Rocks that are made of tiny pieces (sedimentary)
Rocks that were melted (igneous) and volcanoes
Fossil discovery
Mirrors reflect
Working with pumps, siphons and capillary action
Taking note of volume
Evaporation and condensation
Sound is vibration
Making a chemical reaction to create slime
Eating sunlight (outside in sunshine)
Objects in motion
Our sense of touch
Mixing and separating colors
Our sense of smell
Wheels are tools (outside)
Bubbles
Recycling paper to use again
Rocket ships blasting off
Making solutions
Measuring hands

EVERYDAY
Science Lessons

Each science experience has several activities, which, if done in sequence, build on each other. Doing everything from "To Get Ready" to "Follow-Up Activities" will give children repeated opportunities to understand concepts. The individual activities can be used separately, and children often want to repeat their favorite activities.

Using Children's Literature to Teach the Scientific Method:
Encouraging Children to Make Predictions
While Reading a Book

OBJECTIVE
To help preschoolers and their teachers take the first step to using the scientific method

WHAT IS THE SCIENTIFIC METHOD?

The scientific method is a way of figuring out what question to ask, what steps to take to answer that question, then doing our best to make sure that the information gathered is not biased. The scientific method, like manners, can become a habit at an early age by expecting children to come up with questions and then to find answers to those questions.

Following the scientific method entails exploring a situation, focusing on what you think might happen. This is called making a hypothesis or prediction (or in the case of preschoolers, a guess) about what might happen. One way to help children develop the skill of predicting (or guessing) what might happen is to ask them to guess what will happen next when you read them a book. Then follow up by asking them if things turned out the way they thought it would. Make it clear that you want the children to make predictions and that you will respect and accept all answers (and not provide any).

Materials
Fortunately by Remy Charlip

What to Do

1. Any book will do, but *Fortunately* by Remy Charlip is particularly well suited to getting children started thinking about what happens next in a book, noticing patterns, and asking questions.
2. Read the first few pages during story time. Stop after the pattern of alternating happy/sad pages has been repeated two or three times.

♀ Each science experience has several activities, which, if done in sequence, build on each other.
Doing everything from "To Get Ready" to "Follow-Up Activities" will give children repeated opportunities to understand concepts.
The individual activities can be used separately, and children often want to repeat their favorite activities.

3. Ask the children:
   - What do you think will happen next?
   - Will it be a happy page or a sad page? What will he do?
4. Turn the page and find out what does happen. Ask the children:
   - Is it a happy page or a sad page?
   - What is happening?
   - Is this what you thought would happen?

Repeat steps two and three as long as the children are interested.

What to Talk About

1. After children practice the skill of predicting what might happen next when you read books to them, build on this skill during science experiences. After children have explored materials, ask them,
   - What do you think will happen?
   - Why do you think that will happen?
2. Ask other leading questions to help them make predictions and hypotheses. For example:
   - If I throw this ball up to the sky, where do you think it will stop?

   Follow up with:
   - Did it happen the way you thought it would?
3. Give children a chance to say what they think will happen before an activity begins and before adult opinions are voiced. Also give them opportunities to describe what they saw happen, and why they think it happened that way. For example, if the children find a bug on the playground, after you ask them what they think it is, ask:
   - What is it doing?
   - Where did you find it, on the ground, on a bush?

Encourage them to recognize or build their store of knowledge about the bug.

4. At other times, children will want you to act as a source of information for them. When this is clearly what they are looking for, answer the questions or help them research it with you using a book.

Books to Read

Almost any book will do if you remember to ask, "What do you think will happen?"
Fortunately by Remy Charlip
How to Think Like a Scientist: Answering Questions by the Scientific Method by Stephen Kramer, illustrated by Felicia Bond
Suddenly by Colin McNaughton

Website to Visit

www.enc.org/focus/lit–Eisenhower National Clearinghouse, see *Focus,* a magazine that helps educators incorporate children's literature into math and science curricula.

Bringing Science Home!
A Note Home to Families About Reading Books to Your Child to Promote the Scientific Method

Dear Families,

Does preschool seem a little early to be talking about the scientific method? It is never too early to develop children's ability to learn how to ask questions and support their desire to find answers, which is part of the scientific method.

What is the scientific method? It is a way of figuring out what question to ask, what steps to take to answer that question, and then to doing our best to make sure that the information gathered is correct. The scientific method, like manners, can become a habit at an early age.

Following the scientific method means focusing attention on what you think will happen, making a hypothesis or prediction (or in the case of preschoolers, a guess). We can help children learn to do this any time you read to them, by asking them to predict what will happen next in the story. At the end of the story, ask them if things turned out the way they predicted. Be clear that you want your child to predict (or guess) what might happen and that you will respect and accept all answers. Their answers do not have to agree with yours.

Magnets and Testing Hypotheses

Magnets are fascinating to explore. Their power is mysterious to us because we cannot use our senses to figure out how they work. Through repeated exploration preschoolers can become familiar with the action of magnetic force, and realize that it is not like the magic in storybooks that needs a special person or special thing to work. Everyone can use a magnet and the magnet will always attract some objects and not others. Magnetic force operates in predictable ways.

TO GET READY—
Introducing Magnet Play

Materials

variety of magnets—some with handles,
     horseshoe, and bar
objects made of various materials
sorting trays

What to Do

1. To allow children time to form their own ideas, let them explore the properties of magnets, including what types of objects are attracted to magnets. Put magnets, a variety of objects made of different materials, and sorting trays on the science table for children to explore.

2. Ask children about the properties of magnets, such as:
   - How do they attract objects?
   - Do all the magnets attract the same things?
   - What kinds of things do they attract?
   - Will the magnets work in other places, such as the water table or refrigerator?

OBJECTIVES
To experience the force of magnetism
To introduce the concept of making a hypothesis

SCIENCE TABLE
Put a clear container of iron filings and three magnets of different shapes on the Science Table. Keep them out for a few weeks, or as long as you are exploring this experience with the children. The children can move the filings around within the box or put the magnets on top to see the direction of the magnetic field (as seen in the way the filings line up).

ᵱ What are you doing with the magnet?
ᵱ How is that object sticking to the magnet? Did you use glue or tape?
ᵱ What else will be attracted to the magnet?
ᵱ Why are those objects attracted to the magnet?
ᵱ What do you think will happen if we touch the two magnets together?

Feeling Magnetic Force

Materials
doughnut magnets
pencils

What to Do
1. Introduce magnetism by giving each child two doughnut magnets slid onto a pencil so that the force of magnetism pushes them apart.

What to Talk About
1. Ask:
   ᵱ Can you make the two magnets stay together?
   ᵱ What is happening with the magnets?
2. The children will discover many fun ways to manipulate the magnets. Ask:
   ᵱ Can you feel the force of the magnetism when you pull the magnets apart or push them together?
3. One property of magnets is that they attract some objects. Just like one property of water is that it is wet, magnets have magnetic force—the property of attracting some objects to it. The force called magnetism happens when the atoms in the magnet line up. Although we cannot see them lined up, we can experience what happens to objects near the magnet.

Magnets Attract Some Objects

Materials

variety of magnets—some with handles, horseshoe, and bar
assortment of small objects

What to Do

1. Have the children handle a magnet and a variety of small objects. Keys and coins are very popular so include many of these.

What to Talk About

1. Ask:
   - ℗ What kinds of things are attracted to magnets?
2. Encourage the children to group the objects, to generalize about other related objects, and to check if their neighbors are getting the same results. Ask:
   - ℗ Are all the paper clips attracted to the magnets?
3. Explain that a hypothesis is a statement of what we think will happen. Ask the children to make a hypothesis about which types of objects are attracted to the magnet and which are not. Many children say that the magnet will attract the metal or shiny objects. Let them discover if their hypothesis is true by giving them pieces of aluminum foil and brass keys, as well as steel nails and bolts containing iron.

Testing Objects and Making a Hypothesis

Materials

variety of magnets—some with handles, horseshoe, and bar
assortment of objects

What to Do

1. Select an object from a group of many objects made of various materials. Put it in the center of the table.
2. Ask the children to use their words, not their magnets, and say if they think it will be attracted to the magnet or not. You may need to collect their magnets to focus their thinking.
3. Ask one child to test a prediction without comment or correction from you. Repeat as often as necessary or as long as the children are interested.

What to Talk About

1. Ask:
   - ℗ Was that what you thought would happen?
   - ℗ Did you think it (a specific object) would be attracted to the magnet?

More Hypothesizing

Materials

magnets
assortment of objects
poster board or felt board

What to Do

1. Present the children with a select group of small objects without a magnet. Let them handle the objects for a few minutes and then remove them.
2. Ask:
   - ℗ Do you think some of those objects will be attracted to a magnet?
3. Create a poster or felt board picture showing a magnet above a bowl. The poster can be just a piece of cardboard with felt shapes of a magnet at the top and a bowl at the bottom glued to it. Ask each child to make a prediction (guess), based on his or

her earlier hypothesis, of whether the object will be attracted to a magnet. The children record their predictions by placing photocopies of the objects to "attracted" (touching the picture of the magnet) or the "not attracted" position (on the picture of the bowl). Attach the photocopies with tape or pieces of Velcro.

4. After the children have recorded their predictions, test one object at a time by touching a magnet to the actual objects. To help the children focus on testing their hypotheses rather than on who was "right" about a particular object, give the pictures and the corresponding actual objects to different children. With each object, compare their results with their recorded predictions. After testing an object, they may want to move its picture to correspond with the test results if their original prediction was incorrect.

5. As you test each object, ask:
   - Did the object belong in the group you predicted it would?
   - Was your hypothesis correct?
   - Would you like to move the picture of the object?

Follow-Up Activities

- Repeat these experiences in a new way or in a new place by using different objects.
- Play a magnet game, using a magnet tied to a string to fish for paper fish that have paperclip noses. Or, fish for small magnets hidden in the sand table using a large magnet.
- Ask other questions related to hypotheses and predictions.

Books to Read

How to Think Like a Scientist: Answering Questions by the Scientific Method by Stephen Kramer, illustrated by Felicia Bond

Marta's Magnets by Wendy Pfeffer

What Makes a Magnet? by Franklyn M. Branley

Bringing Science Home!
A Note Home to Families About Magnets and Making Predictions

Dear Families,

Playing with magnets is so much fun! Magnetic force is mysterious and seems like magic. Yet, by playing with magnets repeatedly and experiencing how magnets act, children find that magnets are predictable. They act the same way each time with the same object. They learn that, just as water is always wet, a magnet attracts certain objects, those that contain iron (although we can't see that). Before they put a magnet near a new object, children learn to predict whether it will be attracted to the magnet. They are using the scientific method of making a hypothesis (guessing what they think will happen) and testing it. Afterwards we ask, "Was that what you thought would happen?"

Year-Round Gardening

OBJECTIVES

To note the passing of time
To recognize that the four seasons occur sequentially and are a cycle
To connect the change of seasons with a year-long cycle

SCIENCE TABLE

Keep the Seasons' Circle chart where the children can see it each day.

TO GET READY—

Introducing the Seasons

Materials

books about the seasons (see list on page 35)

What to Do

1. For everything there is a season: This introduction shows how gardening/nature lessons can be tied together and recorded in the classroom to make sense of the concept of "a year" and to connect the change of the seasons with a cycle.

2. Read a book that incorporates the seasons or is about seasons. (See book suggestions on page 35.)

⌀ Each science experience has several activities, which, if done in sequence, build on each other.
Doing everything from "To Get Ready" to "Follow-Up Activities" will give children repeated opportunities to understand concepts.
The individual activities can be used separately, and children often want to repeat their favorite activities.

3. Introduce the Seasons' Circle chart (see description below). Keep it where the children can see it and add to it each day.

Participating in Seasonal Changes

Materials
nearby tree

What to Do
1. For each month or season, observe the changes to a nearby tree and do a gardening activity that marks or represents the season. The activities listed below are presented in detail in separate experiences. Record the activities on a "Seasons' Circle" chart (see next activity).
2. Update the chart on a weekly basis.

What to Talk About
1. Ask:
    * Why is this the time of the year to plant a certain plant? (The weather conditions are best for the plant to grow up and make seeds or new plants.)
    * Why are the tree's leaves changing color? (The tree has stopped making the green color, chlorophyll, to get ready to rest over the winter.)
2. In conversation about when events (not necessarily related to seasonal changes) did or will take place, refer to the gardening activities or plant growth observations. For example:
    * When these bulbs bloom, the school year will be half over.
    * You will be six when the leaves fall from this tree (or before the tree grows new leaves).
    * We did that project about the same time we planted the lettuce seeds.
    * Your new baby brother or sister will be born before these pea plants make flowers.

Seasons' Circle

Materials
poster board or large sheet of foam board
markers

What to Do
1. Record the activities on the Seasons' Circle, a circular chart that is sturdy enough to last all year. These "garden happenings" can:
    * be drawn by a child on a separate sheet of paper and then cut out and glued to the chart
    * be drawn by an adult
    * be cutouts from catalogues or the newspaper
    * be actual plant parts, pressed and dried, then glued to the chart
    * contain an appropriate amount of words
2. Some items to include on the Seasons' Circle are strawberry plants (dried), actual tree seeds (apple, maple), cut-out pictures of flowering daffodils, tree leaf rubbings, herb seeds, dried flowers, and children's drawings of their gardens.

What to Talk About
1. Ask:
    * What happened before today (in the garden/outside)?
    * What is happening today?
    * What will happen in the future?

Other Experiences to Use Throughout the Year With Year-Round Gardening:

- Planting Strawberry Plants (pages 37-39)
- What Do Seeds Need to Grow? (pages 41-46)
- Why Do Some Tree Leaves Change Color? (pages 47-50)
- Planting Spring Bulbs (pages 64-67)
- Planting Peas on Presidents' Day (pages 87-91)
- Planting an Herb/Butterfly Garden (pages 117-121)
- Dirt, What Is It? (pages 103-107)
- Eating Sunlight (pages 174-179)

Books to Read

Autumn by Terri Degezelle

A Bear for All Seasons by Diane Marcial Fuchs

Chicken Soup with Rice: A Book of Months by Maurice Sendak

My Mama Had a Dancing Heart by Libba Moore Gray

Pieces: A Year in Poems & Quilts by Anna Grossnickle Hines

When This Box Is Full by Patricia Lillie

Winter: An Alphabet Acrostic by Steven Schnur (author has written one book for each of the four seasons)

The Year at Maple Hill Farm by Alice and Martin Provensen

Season's Circle

Bringing Science Home!
A Note Home to Families About Year-Round Gardening

Dear Families,

Throughout this school year, we will be gardening during each season. We will record each planting on our Seasons' Circle, a circular chart that is a way to help young children note the passage of time. It is a way to make sense of the concept of a year and to connect the change of the seasons with a cycle.

We will observe a nearby tree and do a gardening activity for each month or season, which we will record on our Seasons' Circle chart.

We will talk about why a certain time of the year is the time to plant our plants.

Please come and join us!

Planting Strawberry Plants

SCIENCE TABLE

Put a dried and pressed strawberry plant on the Science Table. Keep it out for a few weeks, or as long as you are exploring this experience with the children. Make available paper and crayons or markers and, if possible, a live strawberry plant so children can draw the parts of a strawberry plant.

TO GET READY—
Exploring the Parts of a Plant

Materials

grass

What to Do

1. Look at grass or other plants growing outdoors.
2. Use the names of plant parts—leaves, stem, root, and so on—in conversations with children.
3. Pull up a small amount of grass including the roots and talk about the parts of the grass plant.

What to Talk About

1. Ask:
    ♀ What is holding the grass plant in the ground?
    Let's see.
    ♀ What do you call these hair-like pieces of the grass plant? (roots)

Strawberry Plants

Materials

strawberry plants
paper
crayons/markers

♀ Each science experience has several activities, which, if done in sequence, build on each other.
Doing everything from "To Get Ready" to "Follow-Up Activities" will give children repeated opportunities to understand concepts.
The individual activities can be used separately, and children often want to repeat their favorite activities.

What to Do

1. Examine some strawberry plants that you have dug out of the dirt.
2. Some of the children may want to draw the parts of the strawberry plant.

What to Talk About

1. Ask:
   - ♀ What are the names of the parts of this plant?

   (The children may only know the name for leaf.) Show them the leaf, the stem, and the flower. (Strawberry plants produce flowers in the spring.)
2. Show them the runner—a special stem that has a baby strawberry plant on the end. (Strawberry plants reproduce in the summer by sending out runners that grow a new plant at the end.)
3. Show them the root.
4. Ask:
   - ♀ Where are the strawberries?
   - ♀ When will the strawberries grow on the plant? (The strawberries will follow the flowers that bloom in spring.)
   - ♀ How are these plants like the grass plants?
   - ♀ How are they different?
5. You may want to let the children discover the information in the following activities as they observe the growth and development of the strawberry plant during the year. Like the parts of our bodies, the parts of a plant each have a special job. The leaves get food from the sun and the stem holds the leaf up to the sun. The flower makes the fruit and the runner sends the new plant out to where there is room to grow. The roots hold the plant in the dirt and bring water from the dirt into the plant.

Measuring the Plant

Materials
strawberry plant(s)
ruler

What to Do

1. Measure the length of the plants, including any runners, using Measuring Hands (see pages 224-225) or a ruler. If you have a particularly long runner, it's fun to see if the plant is longer than the children are tall.

What to Talk About

1. Ask:
   - ♀ Which strawberry plant is the longest?
   - ♀ How long is it?
   - ♀ If we hold it up, will it be longer than you are?

Planting Strawberries

Materials

strawberry plants, 6 or more (Because strawberry plants reproduce every fall by sending out runners that then grow new plants at the end, you may be able to get strawberry plants from a local gardener.)

child-sized plastic trowels or large soup spoons

garden bed or planting container

humus, rich dirt, or potting soil

What to Do

1. Plant the strawberry plants where they will receive about 6 to 10 hours of direct sun each day. Raised beds are ideal; half-barrel planters or even small hanging planters are fine.
2. The idea is to produce a handful of berries, not feed the class. What is important is that the children handle the plants gently, put the roots in the ground, and not throw the dirt. After all the planting is finished, water the plants until the dirt is soaked. (If necessary, re-plant the plants after the children have left for the day.)

What to Talk About

1. Ask:
   - ♀ What part goes into the ground?
   - ♀ How do you know or how can we find out? (We could look at the leaves and roots of other plants and see what part is in the ground and what part is above the ground.)
   - ♀ Will these plants need us to care for them? What do we need to do?

Books to Read

Cook-a-Doodle-Doo! by Janet Stevens and Susan Steven Crummel

The First Strawberries, a Cherokee Story by Joseph Bruchac

Garden by Robert Maass

Good Job, Oliver! by Laurel Molk

The Grey Lady and the Strawberry Snatcher by Molly Bang

Jamberry by Bruce Degen

Length by Henry Pluckrose

The Little Mouse, the Red Ripe Strawberry and the Big Hungry Bear by Don and Audrey Wood

Sweet Strawberries by Phyllis Reynolds Naylor

Follow-Up Activities

- ♀ Eat a strawberry snack in anticipation of your crop.
- ♀ Water the plants and check for growth and change. (Any new leaves, runners, or flowers? Any color change in the leaves or any dead leaves?)
- ♀ Record the changes with a drawing and add to the Season's Circle (see page 34).

Bringing Science Home!
A Note Home to Families About Strawberry Plants

Dear Families,

Often scientific discovery happens when a person is curious about something they have observed. The children have planted strawberry plants and plan to observe them every week to see if they grow and change as the season changes. We hope they will produce strawberries.

When we planted strawberry plants, we noticed the parts of the plant: leaf, stem, roots, and maybe a runner or flower or fruit. Your child is beginning to notice how plants are alike and how they are different. Classifying plants allows us to group our knowledge and understand how plants are related. We're just beginning to do this!

What Do Seeds Need to Grow?

OBJECTIVE
To see the changes in seeds under different conditions, some leading to growth

SCIENCE TABLE
Put the items listed below on the Science Table. Keep them out for a few weeks, or as long as you are exploring this experience with the children.

♀ *Start a seed collection.*

♀ *Put the mung bean sprouts and root growth containers (pages 142-143) on the table for daily observation.*

♀ *Measure and chart the growth of the sprouts and roots by having the children draw a new picture every few days to add to the chart. Comparing the size of the sprout to their littlest finger is an age-appropriate way to measure.*

TO GET READY—
Exploring Seeds

Materials
seeds
window boxes or yogurt cups
drt or potting soil
watering can
birdseed and napkin, optional

What to Do
1. Have the children plant several types of seeds in an outside garden or inside in containers such as window boxes or yogurt cups. They will need gentle watering to keep the soil moist and sunshine to grow tall.
2. Alternatively, a spoonful of mixed birdseed can be sprouted on a damp napkin inside a plastic bag. Keep the bag out of the direct sun to prevent mold growth.

What to Talk About
1. Ask:
   ♀ How long to you think it will be until they sprout?
   ♀ Do the seedlings all look the same?

♀ Each science experience has several activities, which, if done in sequence, build on each other.
Doing everything from "To Get Ready" to "Follow-Up Activities" will give children repeated opportunities to understand concepts.
The individual activities can be used separately, and children often want to repeat their favorite activities.

Sorting Seeds

Materials

seeds and corresponding actual plants or plant
   pictures (Seed packets have pictures on the
   front. Seed companies will send a free
   catalogue full of pictures.)
sorting bowls

What to Do

1. Look at a small amount of a mixture of
   seeds (corn, pea, bean, and wheat seeds are
   large enough to easily see the differences).
2. Sort them into separate containers.
3. Look at and try to match the seeds with the
   grown plants or pictures of them.

What to Talk About

1. Ask:
   ♀ What are seeds? (Each seed has a baby
      plant in it; a particular kind of plant. And
      just as puppies only grow up to be
      dogs, and chicken eggs hatch out into
      baby chickens, each seed will grow up
      into the kind of plant that it is.)
   ♀ What do seeds need to grow? (Suggest
      water and sunshine if the children can't
      answer the question.)

Setting Up an Experiment

Materials

mung bean seeds (These are available in Chinese
   groceries or health food sections of grocery
   stores. You can also substitute other small,
   fast-growing sprouts.)
3 plastic containers (clear lids are helpful)

What to Do

1. Have the children make three environments
   with differing amounts of water to try to
   grow mung bean sprouts:
   ♀ Dry container (no water)
   ♀ "Some water" container (½" water,
      barely covering the seeds)
   ♀ "Lots of water" container (fill container
      halfway to the top with water)
Put labels on the three environments with
pictures showing the container with the
seeds and the different amounts of water in
blue.
Yogurt cups with clear lids work well; the
lids keep the moisture in.

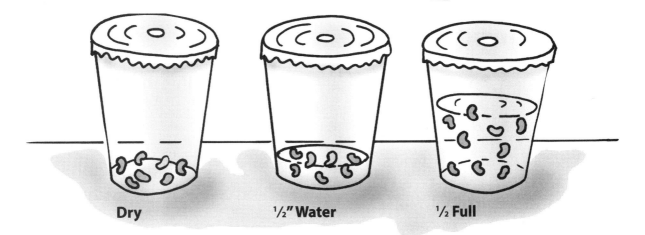

Dry   **½" Water**   **½ Full**

2. Let each child put a seed in each container until there are about 20 seeds. It works best if the children add the water last. Look for results the following week (see "Results of the Experiment" below).

What to Talk About

1. Ask:
   - How long until they sprout?
   - Will they all sprout?
   - How much water do the seeds need to grow well?
   - Which group of seeds do you think will sprout and grow the best?

   The children will have their own ideas about what types of conditions to create for their seeds. Create these additional environments and observe what happens.

Results of the Experiment

What to Do

1. After several days to a week, compare the mung bean seeds/sprouts in the three containers. Unless you have discussed evaporation, you may want to add water up to the original levels (before the children view it) to replace any lost by evaporation.

What to Talk About

1. Ask:
   - In which container do the mung bean sprouts look the happiest or have grown the best? (It will be obvious. The dry ones will not have sprouted, and the one with lots of water—the drowned seeds—will be small and somewhat brown, and may have fermented. The ones with some water—damp seeds—will be biggest and greenest.)
   - How much water did the seeds need to grow well?

Snacking on Bean Sprouts

Materials
mung bean sprouts (the bean sprouts used in Chinese cooking)

What to Do

1. Eat a snack of bean sprouts, either purchased from the grocery or sprouted in the classroom. Rinse well before serving.

What to Talk About

1. Ask:
   - What do the bean sprouts look like?
   - Where is the seed?
   - Where is the sprout?

Planting Inside

Materials
clear plastic jars
paper towels
presoaked bean or corn seeds

What to Do
1. Stuff a clear plastic jar with paper towels.
2. Add enough water to dampen all of the paper towels.
3. Have the children "plant" the seeds in between the clear jar wall and the paper towels so they are visible from the outside.
4. Over a seven-day period, look for root development and keep the paper towels damp.
5. After some root growth, turn jar upside down and watch over several days as the roots change direction to continue growing down.
6. Look at the beans or corn in the jar daily. Watch for root development.

What to Talk About

1. Ask:
   - ❦ Do you think any change will happen to the seeds?
   - ❦ What will grow first: the sprout or the root?
   - ❦ Which way will they grow: up or down?

2. After observing for a few days or a week, ask:
   - ❦ What are roots for?
   - ❦ What would happen to the roots of a plant if they grew up? (Do the children understand that there wouldn't be water available to the roots if they grew into the air?)

3. Sing "I'm a Little Seed" by Carol L. Van Hise to the tune of "I'm a Little Teapot."

   I'm a little seed deep in the ground (stoop down, wrap arms around knees)
   You planted me so that's where I'm found.
   With the rain and sun I start to sprout (gesture raindrops with fingers and the sun with hands over head)
   First my roots, then my leaves come out! (stand and stretch arms up.)

   Carol L. Van Hise, lyrics of song, I'm a Little Seed from *For Two Year Olds* . Used with permission from Carson-Dellosa Publishing Company's CD-0215, *Learning for Little Ones, Seasonal Activities for 2-year olds* © Carson-Dellosa Publishing.

Books to Read

All About Seeds by Melvin Berger
Bean and Plant by Christine Back and Barrie Watts
Grandpa's Garden Lunch by Judith Caseley
How a Seed Grows by Helene J. Jordan
I'm a Seed by Jean Marzollo
A Seed Is a Promise by Claire Merrill
Seeds by George Shannon
The Surprise Garden by Zoe Hall

Bringing Science Home!
A Note Home to Families About What Seeds Need to Grow

Dear Families,

Like scientists, young children try to answer the questions that come to their minds. Seeds are small packages that inspire many questions, including:

- *What are seeds?*
- *What do seeds need to grow?*
- *How long until they sprout?*
- *Will they all sprout?*
- *How can we find out?*

By sprouting a variety of seeds we are finding out that each seed has a baby plant in it, a particular kind of plant. And just as puppies only grow up to be dogs and chicken's eggs hatch out into baby chickens, each type of seed will grow up into one kind of plant. Planting one kind of seed in a variety of conditions may answer some of the questions. Ask your children about the results of experiments!

Why Do Some Tree Leaves Change Color?

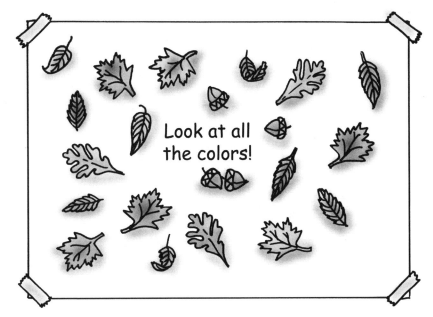

Look at all the colors!

OBJECTIVE
To inform children about leaf color changes in autumn

SCIENCE TABLE
Before leaves become dried out and brittle, display a leaf collection of every color available locally. Ask the children to contribute to the collection. Tape a sheet of clear contact paper to the wall, sticky side out. Children can stick their leaves to the contact paper for display. Keep these items out for a few weeks, or as long as you are exploring this experience with the children.

TO GET READY—
Exploring Leaves Changing Colors

Materials
books about leaves changing colors, such as:
   Autumn Leaves by Ken Robbins
   How Leaves Change by Sylvia A. Johnson
   Red Leaf, Yellow Leaf by Lois Ehlert
fall leaves of many colors

What to Do
1. Read any of the suggested books or another book about changing leaves.
2. Collect fallen leaves from the schoolyard.
3. Make sure the children collect some from your class' special tree (see page 51).

♀ Each science experience has several activities, which, if done in sequence, build on each other.
Doing everything from "To Get Ready" to "Follow-Up Activities" will give children repeated opportunities to understand concepts.
The individual activities can be used separately, and children often want to repeat their favorite activities.

4. Collect non-deciduous leaves, such as pine needles. (Only the teacher should remove leaves from a tree.)

What to Talk About

1. Ask:

    ◊ Have you seen any leaves that are not green?
    ◊ What colors have you seen?
    ◊ Have you seen a leaf that is the color of these pants? (Refer to colored objects or clothing if the children do not know color names.)

Comparing Leaf Shapes

Materials
fall leaves of many colors

What to Do

1. Encourage the children to look at and touch the leaf collection.
2. Sing the following to the tune of "The More We Get Together."

The Leaves Are Changing Color
Tree leaves are colored green, with chlorophyll, with chlorophyll,
Tree leaves are colored green with chlorophyll pigment.

The chlorophyll is fading, is fading, is fading,
The color green is fading and new ones appear.

The leaves are changing colors, from green to brown,
The leaves are changing colors from green to red.

*The chlorophyll is staying, in some plants
called evergreens,
The chlorophyll is staying and its color is
green.*

What to Talk About

1. Ask:
   - Do you have a favorite leaf?
   - Which types/shapes of tree leaves did you find on the ground and which did you find still on the tree? (Deciduous trees are ones that lose their leaves in the fall.)

Matching the Leaf Color

Materials

fall leaves of many colors
red, yellow, and green plastic or acetate

What to Do

1. Give each child small pieces of green, red, and yellow acetate (plastic or acetate can be purchased from craft or artist supply stores, or clear plastic wrapping paper from party stores).
2. The children will discover that if they overlap them, the colors combine to match the leaf colors.

What to Talk About

1. Ask:
   - What plants are a green color? (Chlorophyll is the green color in plants, a pigment. It is a tool that plants use to catch sunlight to make food.)
   - Do we have chlorophyll in us?

- Which kind of leaves are green/red/yellow/orange/brown?
- What colors of acetate do you need to overlap to make those colors? (Chlorophyll covers up the yellow and orange pigments in the leaves. When the tree stops making food in the fall to get ready to rest in the winter, it stops making chlorophyll and then the yellow and orange, that were there all the time, can be seen. The red colors form when lots of sunlight changes the sugar left in the leaf to a red pigment. If a leaf has little sugar, it turns brown.)

Books to Read

Autumn Leaves by Ken Robbins
Fresh Fall Leaves by Betsy Franco
How Leaves Change by Sylvia A. Johnson
Red Leaf, Yellow Leaf by Lois Ehlert
Trees, Leaves and Bark, Take-Along Guide by Daniel L. Burns

Follow-Up Activities

- Use the word *chlorophyll*. (Who is wearing the color of chlorophyll today?)
- Add to the leaf collection.
- Check the class' special tree to see if there have been any changes.

Bringing Science Home!
A Note Home to Families About Why Some Leaves Change Color

Dear Families,
Sometimes children ask us questions about nature whose answers are not easy to demonstrate but must be explained in words instead of children's exploration. As children get older, they will add their yearly observations together to build an understanding of nature. Meanwhile, here are a few answers to the question of why some tree leaves change colors in the fall.

For three-year-olds:
Not much water is available to trees in the winter so some trees need to rest and not grow new leaves until spring. The yellow, orange, red, and brown colors come when the green color (chlorophyll) goes away.

For some fours and fives:
Not much water is available to trees in the winter because the ground becomes frozen. So some trees need to rest. They stop sending water to their leaves so the leaves will drop. That keeps the water inside the tree trunk and branches, and keeps the tree alive. When the leaves stop getting water, the green color, chlorophyll, fades away and then you can see the yellow and orange, which was there all the time. The red colors form when lots of sunlight changes the sugar left in the leaf to a red color. If a leaf has just a little bit of sugar it turns brown. The trees will grow new leaves in the spring.

Stretch Your Senses on a Walk to a Nearby Park

BIG TREE

Before the Walk

Materials

gloves
trash bag

What to Do

1. The day before visiting the park or area where there are trees, check out the area around the tree and clean up any dangerous trash. Also, check for any natural hazards such as poison ivy, mushrooms, rough terrain, or water so you can prepare the group ahead of time to avoid these hazards.

TO GET READY—

Exploring a Class Tree

Materials

tree identification book
tree in a nearby park
paper, pen, and tape

What to Do

1. Have each class befriend a nearby tree to visit on a weekly or monthly basis.
2. Use an identification book to discover the name of the tree. Alternatively, the children could give it a name that identifies one of its characteristics such as the "big" tree, the "smooth-bark" tree, or the tree "with the heart-shaped leaves."

OBJECTIVE
To introduce children to the many parts of a park

SCIENCE TABLE
Ask each child to contribute one nature find to the Science Table. Glue leaves flat on paper or press them to make their shapes easier to see. Put these items on the Science Table. Keep them out for a few weeks, or as long as you are exploring this experience with the children.

Each science experience has several activities, which, if done in sequence, build on each other.
Doing everything from "To Get Ready" to "Follow-Up Activities" will give children repeated opportunities to understand concepts.
The individual activities can be used separately, and children often want to repeat their favorite activities.

3. Make a label to tape to the trunk or post nearby (puncturing the bark with nails or tacks might allow insects and disease into the tree).

4. Throughout the year notice any changes in the tree, looking at the trunk, leaves, and branches. You could add this to the calendar or job list.

On the Walk

Materials

collection bag (clear, zipper-closure bags work well) for each child (labeled with each child's name ahead of time)

large illustrations or drawings of common trees' leaf shapes in the local area (trace these or make rubbings from the actual leaves you will see on your walk the week before you take the children)

large-size crayons and paper for tree bark rubbings

small trowel or spoon for the teacher to dig with

tree and insect identification books

first aid kit

trash bag and gloves

safety instructions for teacher's helpers (see next page)

What to Do

1. Take the entire class on a walking field trip to a nearby natural area or park. Avoid one with playgrounds so that you can concentrate on the natural parts of the park.

2. At the park, discover different leaf shapes, tall plants, short plants, the smells of leaves, and other experiences that the park offers. **Note:** Be sure that the children do not touch poisonous plants such as poison ivy and mushrooms.

3. Encourage the children to put nature finds into the zipper-closure plastic bags with their names on them.

CAUTION: Do not collect any mushrooms or poisonous plants. Leave behind anything too big for the bag (most likely sticks or rocks).

4. Make tree bark rubbings. Hold a sheet of thin paper up to the tree while the children take turns rubbing a thick crayon over it to reveal and record the texture. These can go in the children's bags. Some children will want to make many rubbings.

5. Lie on the ground under a tree and look up. Comment on the branch pattern.

6. Sing the following song to the tune of "Skip to My Lou."

Crinkle, crinkle, crunchity crunch,
Crinkle, crinkle, crunchity crunch,
Crinkle, crinkle, crunchity crunch,
I love autumn leaves a bunch!
(Reprinted from Totline Sept/Oct 1994 by permission of The McGraw-Hill Companies.)

Or for the ambitious and strong-lunged, sing the old favorite memory challenger "The Green Grass Grew All Around" (rewritten for trees).

Oh in the park,
There was a tree,
The biggest oak tree,
That you ever did see....(chorus)

And on that oak,
There was a limb (branch, twig, leaf),
The very best limb,
That you ever did see....(chorus)

Chorus
And the autumn leaves fell all around, all around,
And the autumn leaves fell all around.

What to Talk About

1. Ask questions about parks, such as why the children like them and why parks are good.
2. Other subjects are the cycle of seasons, the shapes of natural things, seeing the park as a whole with many parts: the ground (dirt, soil), under the ground (roots, insects), what grows in the ground (small plants, tall plants), above the ground (the sky, animals, birds, and so on).
3. Ask:
   - What is on the ground? In the ground? Under logs?
   - How does the tree bark feel?
   - Do all trees have the same bark texture?
4. Ask the children for their ideas on the nature around you. Share their excitement in discovering the feel of tree bark, the smell of dirt, and the beauty of nature.

Books to Read

Autumn Leaves by Ken Robbins
Good Mushrooms and Bad Toadstools by Allan Fowler
I Wonder (Green Light Readers) by Tana Hoban
A Log's Life by Wendy Pfeffer
Looking Down by Steve Jenkins
Meeting Trees by Scott Russell Sanders
Red Leaf, Yellow Leaf by Lois Ehlert
A Tree Is Nice by Janice May Udry

Follow-Up Activities

- Use shapes from a tangram to make certain leaf shapes that the children found at the park. (A tangram is an ancient Chinese puzzle containing seven pieces. It has five triangles, one parallelogram, and one square. These geometric shapes can be made from art foam.)

SAFETY INSTRUCTIONS FOR TEACHER'S HELPERS

Safety rules to observe to and from the park:
- *Stick together with your assigned children.*
- *Stay on the sidewalk when walking to and from the park.*
- *Adults walk on the street-side of the sidewalk, children on the inside.*
- *Keep children away from trash, especially broken glass and other dangerous items, and poisonous plants such as poison ivy and mushrooms.*
- *Use gloves and trash bags as needed.*

- Compare the leaves from the park to the class tree.
- Make rubbings, prints, or collages using the nature finds, such as leaves, acorns, pieces of bark, or other objects, in the children's bags. Make a collage that represents the parts of the park by gluing objects found in the park to a piece of stiff cardboard or by sticking them to a sheet of contact paper.

Bringing Science Home!
A Note Home to Families About Exploring a Park

Dear Families,

Did you ever lie down under a tree and look up at the way its branches radiate from the trunk? While you are down there, you can smell the ground and maybe see a tiny insect, such as an ant, going about its business. When exploring a park, you may find many interesting objects, such as pieces of trees that have fallen to the ground. Maybe some came home with your child today.

The park we visited has many parts, including the ground and all the roots and insects in it, the plant life big and small, animals and insects such as beetles and squirrels, and the sky with birds and clouds.

We marched back to school while singing this tune (to the tune of "Skip to My Lou"):

Crinkle, crinkle, crunchity crunch,
Crinkle, crinkle, crunchity crunch,
Crinkle, crinkle, crunchity crunch,
I love autumn leaves a bunch!
(Permission granted from Totline Sept/Oct 1994)

Crickets and Using Magnifiers

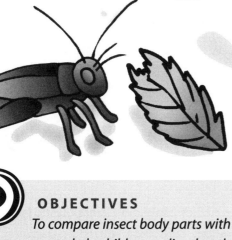

TO GET READY—

Exploring Insects

Materials

insects or books about insects, such as:
> *It's a Good Thing There Are Insects* by
> Alan Fowler
> > *"Leave That Cricket Be, Alan Lee"*
> by Barbara Ann Porte
> *Squash It!* by Eric A. Kimmel
> *The Very Quiet Cricket* by Eric Carle

What to Do

1. Show the children insects in the schoolyard or in books, being sure to use the word "insect."

Using Magnifiers

Materials

variety of magnifiers
variety of objects to examine, such as cloth, feathers, hair, and dead insects

What to Do

1. Have the children practice using a variety of magnifiers to examine the details of a variety of objects. Provide feathers and scraps of different cloths to view.
2. Ask:
   - What do the magnifiers have in common?

OBJECTIVES
To compare insect body parts with our own to help children realize that there is not a one-to-one correspondence
To introduce the use of a magnifying glass

SCIENCE TABLE
Put crickets on the Science Table for the children to observe for several days. Feed them tiny amounts of dog food and fresh fruits. Record the children's observations. Have they been eating? How can you tell? (Poop) Do any of the crickets chirp? When? Release the crickets outside when the class is finished observing them. For additional information about caring for insects, read Pet Bugs and More Pet Bugs *by Sally Kneidel.*

Each science experience has several activities, which, if done in sequence, build on each other.
Doing everything from "To Get Ready" to "Follow-Up Activities" will give children repeated opportunities to understand concepts.
The individual activities can be used separately, and children often want to repeat their favorite activities.

How do they look and feel?

3. Suggest that the children pinch their fingers over the clear part and move them from one side to the other. (The lenses are clear, not flat but curved in some way).

What to Talk About

1. By moving the magnifier closer to yourself and then farther away, you can find the point where you can see best. Move the lens too close and what you see looks fuzzy. Children love to put the magnifier right up to their eyes to see those huge magnified eyes. Move the lens too far away and everything looks fuzzy. Somewhere in the middle is a clear image. Many children are not ready to view clearly and steadily through a magnifier until they are four or older. Do not insist that they use them the "correct" way.

Looking at Insects

Materials

large drawing of cricket body parts
illustrations of crickets (from insect books)
magnifiers
dead crickets in clear containers (optional)

What to Do

1. Have each child look at illustrations of crickets using the magnifying glasses (to practice with the magnifiers again).

2. Have the children name the body parts on a large illustration of a cricket.

3. If possible, introduce the dead insects in clear containers, and examine them using the magnifiers to see details.

What to Talk About

1. Ask:
   - How many legs do the insects have?
   - Do you see any eyes, ears, or mouth?
   - Do you see any parts that people don't have? (Point out the antennae and that insects have six legs.)

Introducing Live Crickets

Materials

three cricket containers (clear plastic jars work well)
four crickets per container (if you don't want to collect them yourself, they can be purchased from pet stores)
dog food and fresh fruit to feed the crickets
insect identification books

What to Do

1. Tell the children that you will show them some live crickets and that the crickets are in a container and cannot get out. Then introduce the live insects.

2. Look at three kinds of crickets, if all three can be collected: field, wood, and camelback (or cave) crickets.

3. Observe as the insects jump and eat. Do they move their antennae? The children may want you to write down their observations.

4. Introduce insect identification books.

What to Talk About

1. Ask:
   - What is in each container? (We have more than one kind of cricket in our part of the world. We can learn many things by watching/observing them.)
   - How are the kinds of crickets different from each other?

- Where have you seen them?
- Where do they live?
- What do they eat?
- How do they make noise? (Male crickets make the chirping noise by rubbing their wings together. The vibrations make the sound.)
- What are those pokey things sticking out from their bottoms? (The crunchy part of a cricket, for those who have stepped on one, is the outside of its body, is its skeleton and is made of chitin. Females have a long ovipositor sticking out from their bottom in addition to the two smaller creces present on both sexes. They poke it into the ground to lay their eggs in a safe place.)

Books to Read

Use magnifiers to see the insects' details while reading these books:
It's a Good Thing There Are Insects by Alan Fowler
"Leave That Cricket Be, Alan Lee" by Barbara Ann Porte
The Very Quiet Cricket by Eric Carle

About other small insects:
Compost Critters by Bianca Lavies
More Pet Bugs by Sally Stenhouse Kneidel
Pet Bugs by Sally Stenhouse Kneidel
Squash It! by Eric A. Kimmel

And for adults, a wonderful book about the lives of insects:
Broadsides from the Other Orders: A Book of Bugs by Sue Hubbell

Follow-Up Activity

- Learn the following song to point out that insect body parts do not correspond one to one with human body parts. Sing to the tune of "Head, Shoulders, Knees and Toes" and gesture to the pretend body part:
  Head, thorax, ab-do-men, abdomen. (The insect's thorax is the part where the limbs are attached—point to your chest. The insect's abdomen is the part after the legs are attached—point to your bottom.)
  Head, thorax, ab-do-men, abdomen.
  Eyes, antenna, and mouth and palps, (Point to your mouth, then make your index fingers into tiny arms at your mouth to be the palps, which are mouth parts.)
  Head, thorax, ab-do-men, abdomen.

Bringing Science Home!
A Note Home to Families About Crickets and Using Magnifiers

Dear Families,
We used magnifying glasses to look closely at crickets. It takes practice to find just the right distance between the lens of the magnifying glass and the object for good viewing. We noticed that crickets have six legs, which makes them insects.

Here's a song we learned about insect body parts. Sing it to the tune of "Head, Shoulders, Knees and Toes" and gesture to the pretend body part:

Head, thorax, ab-do-men, abdomen.
(The insect's thorax is the part where the limbs are attached—point to your chest. The insect's abdomen is the part after the legs are attached—point to your bottom.)
Head, thorax, ab-do-men, abdomen.
Eyes, antenna, and mouth and palps,
(Point to your mouth, then make your index fingers into tiny arms at your mouth to be the palps, which are mouth parts.)
Head, thorax, ab-do-men, abdomen.

Even if you don't like insects you can read about them in a good book called It's a Good Thing There Are Insects *by Alan Fowler.*

Compost Critters

OBJECTIVES

To observe the habits of commonly found small animals such as slugs, earthworms, millipedes, and "roly-poly" bugs (tiny crustaceans also known as sow bugs or pill bugs)

To classify such animals based on observations

SCIENCE TABLE

Put the following items on your Science Table. Keep them out for a few weeks, or as long as you are exploring this experience with the children.

♀ The small animal habitat (see pages 60-61)

♀ Materials to draw pictures of the animals

A sketch notebook with a spiral binding is a good way to keep all the observations together. A child may dictate observations for an adult to record in the same notebook. You may want to date the drawings and writings so you can refer back to them later in the year when the size or number of animals has grown.

TO GET READY—

Exploring Small Animals

Talk about animals of all sizes and what they need in order to live. Asking about pets is a good way to stimulate the discussion. What are the largest and the smallest animals you know of? How do you know they are animals?

Discovering Small Animals

Materials

none needed

What to Do

1. Take the children on a "small animal hunt" around the school grounds or neighborhood.
2. Look for small creatures such as slugs, earthworms, millipedes, and roly-poly bugs (also known as sow bugs or pill bugs), most of which can be found in damp places.
3. Look under leaf piles or rocks, around stacks of bricks, and under dead branches or logs on the ground. Be sure to replace the coverings.

What to Talk About

1. Ask:
   ♀ If we were to invite some of these animals to visit us in the classroom, what would we need to prepare for them so they would be comfortable? (A place to hide under, dirt, a stick, some leaves, food.)
   You may have to point out the dampness of their habitat if the children do not notice it.

♀ Each science experience has several activities, which, if done in sequence, build on each other. Doing everything from "To Get Ready" to "Follow-Up Activities" will give children repeated opportunities to understand concepts. The individual activities can be used separately, and children often want to repeat their favorite activities.

Finding Information in an Identification Book

Materials

books to identify small animals, including:

Backyard Pets: Activities for Exploring Wildlife Close to Home by Carol A. Amato

Compost Critters by Bianca Lavies

Creepy Crawlies and the Scientific Method: More Than 100 Hands-On Science Experiments for Children by Sally Kneidel

Insects: A Guide to Familiar American Insects (Golden Guide) by Herbert Spencer Zim et al

Insects (National Audobon Society First Field Guides) by Christina Wilsdon

It's a Good Thing There Are Insects by Allan Fowler

Peterson First Guide to Insects of North America by Rodger Tory Peterson

What to Do

1. Use an identification book (see book suggestions above) to find the names of the animals you saw on the "small animal hunt." You may need several because these animals belong to different groups, such as mollusk (slugs and snails), crustacean (roly-polies), and insect (beetles).

What to Talk About

1. Say, "We saw animals in the slug family, the worm family, the roly-poly family, and the millipede family. Let's see if the books tell us what these animals eat."

Creating a Small Animal Habitat

Materials

a container to make a habitat

natural materials

small bugs from the schoolyard or neighborhood

CAUTION: Do not include centipedes because they may have a painful bite.

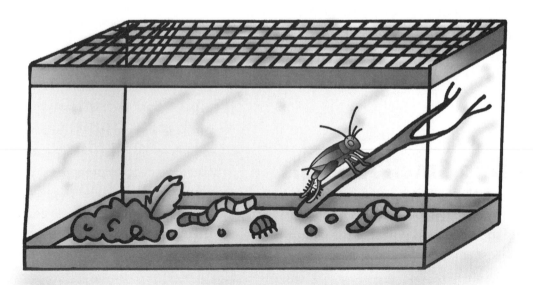

What to Do

1. Work with the children to set up a home or habitat for some of the small animals you found outside under leaves and stones, in the garden, or around the school building. Any container will work as long as it has clear sides for viewing, lets in light, is waterproof so it won't leak, and has a lid that will let air pass through but not small fingers or insects.

2. A snack food container, such as a clear, empty, plastic pretzel jar or cookie container, can be recycled into a terrarium. Wash thoroughly, and then punch some air holes or use a large piece of foam sponge cut to fit the opening the same as a lid. (The sponge in the lid will allow air to pass through.)

3. Encourage the children to include sand, dirt from outside, a stick from the ground, a few small rocks or pieces of bark, and some dead leaves. A small live plant can also be included.

What to Talk About

1. Ask:
   - What else will the small animals need to live?
   - What can we feed them?
   - How long will they visit our classroom? (Two weeks is the minimum for the children to have sufficient time to make observations of these slow-moving and sometimes shy animals. You can keep the habitats over winter, but eventually release the animals in the spring because the wastes of even small animals do build up in a closed system with no rain to cleanse it.)

Observing the Small Animals

Materials

container and animals from previous activity

What to Do

1. Maintain the habitat and observe the animals.

2. The habitat must be kept moist, but at the same time, the dirt and sand should not be soaked or the animals could drown. A spray mist bottle can deliver an appropriate amount of water.

3. Feed them with small pieces of carefully washed lettuce, kale or collards, carrots, or any fresh foods that the children are having for snack that day. They also eat dead leaves, especially maple leaves. Remove the food if it gets moldy.

What to Talk About

1. Ask:
   - What are the animals doing?
   - Are they eating?
   - Where do they like to be?
   - How many legs do they have?
   - Can you see any eyes?

Follow-Up Activities

- Provide the materials for the children to plant a few seeds of lettuce, any type of greens, or beans in a small amount of dirt in a small paper cup. When the seeds begin to sprout and grow a few leaves, cut away the sides of the cup and put the plants into the habitat for a tasty snack for your guests.

- Sprout a turnip root in a cup of water and feed its leaves to your animal guests. Use a clear cup to hold the turnip so the children can observe root growth, as well.

- It is common for the small animals in the habitat to be referred to as "bugs." Promote the use of the individual names, such as millipede, earthworm, roly-poly, and slug, rather than promote the misconception that all tiny animals are in the insect class of the animal kingdom. Here is a chant to help the children learn the scientific names of some animal groups. You or they can point to the animals as you say the chant.

> **Little Animals**
> *Arthropod, crustacean, roly-poly too,*
> *All these names belong to you!*
>
> *Arthropod, diplopod, millipede too,*
> *All these names belong to you!*
>
> *Mollusk, gastropod, slug (or snail) too!*
> *All these names belong to you!*
>
> *Arthropod, insect, springtail too,*
> *All these names belong to you!*
>
> *Annelid, lumbricid, earthworm too,*
> *All these names belong to you!*

Books to Read

The book that inspired this lesson is:
Compost Critters by Bianca Lavies

Another good book is:
Pet Bugs: A Kid's Guide to Catching and Keeping Touchable Insects by Sally Kneidel

For additional information on setting up and maintaining the habitat:
Creepy Creepy Crawlies and the Scientific Method: More Than 100 Hands-On Science Experiments for Children by Sally Kneidel

Bringing Science Home!
A Note Home to Families About Observing Small Animals

Dear Families,

Commonly found creatures such as slugs, earthworms, millipedes, and "roly-polies" are a safe introduction to the many kinds of animals in the world. We have been observing them up close to begin to classify them based on observations of their body shapes and habits. The children have been watching these little creatures repeatedly while they live in a container in our classroom. Already, the children have noticed that the slugs are sticky and the roly-poly bugs (tiny crustaceans also known as sow bugs or pill bugs), curl up into balls when touched. Come in and see our small animal habitat.

Spring–Flowering Bulbs... Are Planted in the Fall

OBJECTIVES
To learn about cycles in nature
To note the sequence of the seasons

SCIENCE TABLE
Plant an amaryllis or paperwhite bulb and observe its growth. Ask, "Where does its food come from?" (Water, the dirt, and the sun nourish the plant. Some food is stored inside the bulb. Last summer when the plant had leaves, its chlorophyll made extra food and stored it in the bulb. Just like with seeds that sprout, the amaryllis roots grow first.) Ask the children to guess which way the roots will grow. Will we see them above the dirt? (After the roots grow, the flower bud sprouts up, and then the leaves appear.) Put the bulbs on the Science Table. Keep them out for a few weeks, or as long as you are exploring this experience with the children.

TO GET READY—
Exploring Spring-Flowering Bulbs

Materials
books about bulbs, such as *Planting a Rainbow* by Lois Ehlert

What to Do
1. Read *Planting a Rainbow* by Lois Ehlert, which shows bulbs in the ground before sprouting and when blooming. Or, read any cycle-of-the-seasons books, such as:

   Be Blest: A Celebration of the Seasons by Mary Beth Owens

   Spring: An Alphabet Acrostic by Steven Schnur

Each science experience has several activities, which, if done in sequence, build on each other.
Doing everything from "To Get Ready" to "Follow-Up Activities" will give children repeated opportunities to understand concepts.
The individual activities can be used separately, and children often want to repeat their favorite activities.

2. Act out the following song while you sing it to the tune of "Jack in the Box":

Spring flowering bulb, (children curl face down on floor, hiding face)
So safe in the ground,
Way down inside, your little dirt mound, (hands curve over head)
Spring flowering bulb so quiet and still,
Won't you sprout up? (heads up and jump up, stretch arms up high)
Of course I will!

Introducing Spring-Flowering Bulbs

Materials
spring-flowering bulbs such as daffodil, iris, or crocuses (enough for each child to plant one)
pictures of the plants that grow from the bulbs
small trowels or large spoons
one large shovel or pitchfork
hand-washing supplies

What to Do
1. Have each child pick out a bulb. Ask:
   - What is it?
2. Together, look at the bulb shape. Ask:
   - Which end do you think will grow up? (The pointy end)
   - Why is it so big and not small like a seed? (It has food stored in it to feed the plant when it first starts growing, late in winter.)
3. Look at photos of the leaves and flowers that the bulbs will produce.
4. Cut one bulb in half to see if the flower is there yet. (It grows later.)
5. Find a "good spot" to plant. This can be any nook or cranny near the school or in a real flowerbed.

Note: If you live in an area that does not have several months of cold temperatures (below 40 degrees, off and on), the bulbs must be kept in the refrigerator for eight weeks before planting to "fool" them into blooming. These bulbs will begin to grow roots and will sprout as soon as they are removed from the refrigerator and planted.

6. Look at the dirt while digging and notice the texture. It's plant food!
7. Wash hands after planting.
8. Planting bulbs is a good investment because spring-flowering bulbs grow and bloom spring after spring for years, sometimes multiplying.

What to Talk About

1. To everything, there is a season. The bulb is not a seed but it is like a seed in that it will grow into a particular kind of plant when it has the right conditions (everything it needs to grow well).

2. Ask:

    ⸙ What do you think the bulb needs to grow well? (To be surrounded by loose dirt, watered, and sunshine. Most bulbs also need to have a cold time for resting.)

    ⸙ When do you think these bulbs will sprout? (In the spring, BUT we don't have to give the children this information. We can encourage them to look for signs of growth at the spot where they planted the bulbs.)

Books to Read

Be Blest: A Celebration of the Seasons by Mary Beth Owens
Planting a Rainbow by Lois Ehlert
Spring: An Alphabet Acrostic by Steven Schnur
To Everything by Bob Barner
When This Box Is Full by Patricia Lillie

Follow-Up Activities

⸙ Record the planting on a Seasons' Circle (see Seasons' Circle lesson on page 34) with pictures cut from a bulb catalogue.

⸙ Keep an eye out for bulb leaves sprouting. Some previously planted bulbs may poke up before the end of winter (late January) and the new ones in early spring (early March).

Bringing Science Home!

A Note Home to Families About Spring Flowering Bulbs That Are Planted in the Fall

Dear Families,

Daffodils, crocus, tulips, and iris flowers bloom from bulbs planted in the fall. We have been exploring flowering bulbs. Each child held a bulb and felt for the pointy end so they could plant it pointy side up. We cut one bulb open but didn't see any flowers inside it. Through our observations, we will answer the question of when flowers will bloom from our bulbs. As we wait for spring, the class will keep checking the spot where we planted our bulbs, watching for any sign that they are growing.

Inside we'll be watching an amaryllis bulb for signs of growth. The children may want to draw what they see. They are wondering which part will grow and when the flower will bloom.

Corn and an Introduction to the Globe

TO GET READY—
Exploring Corn

Materials
corn kernels (seeds from a packet or a cob of dried corn)
plastic bag
paper towels

What to Do
1. Sprout about 10 corn kernels 4 days in advance by putting some seeds in a plastic bag with a damp paper towel and sealing it. Keep it out of direct sunlight to prevent mold growth.

Tell the Story of People and Corn

Materials
Corn Is Maize by Aliki

What to Do
1. Start a discussion by asking:
   ♀ Who likes to eat corn?
2. Then tell the first part of the history of corn as told in *Corn Is Maize* by Aliki (or read selected portions).

What to Talk About
1. A long time ago, people living in Mexico began to grow corn for the very first time.

OBJECTIVES
To introduce the concept of a globe representing where we live—a ball-shaped place—and to relate the globe to a photograph of the Earth

SCIENCE TABLE
Put corn that is sprouting and varieties of dried corn on the Science Table. Keep it out for a few weeks, or as long as you are exploring this experience with the children.

♀ Each science experience has several activities, which, if done in sequence, build on each other. Doing everything from "To Get Ready" to "Follow-Up Activities" will give children repeated opportunities to understand concepts. The individual activities can be used separately, and children often want to repeat their favorite activities.

They took seeds from the wild corn and planted them in their gardens. No one else in the whole world grew it yet. At first, the corn ears were tiny but as the people farmed corn for many years, they learned to grow larger and larger ears of corn. When their neighbors saw that the corn tasted good and helped the people be healthy and strong, they decided to grow it, too. By the time Europeans traveled to the Americas, many people were growing corn.

Touch Corn Seeds

Materials
loose corn kernels
sprouted kernels

What to Do
1. Pass around and examine a corn kernel and a sprouted corn kernel (see Science Table, page 68).

What to Talk About
1. Ask:
   - What do you think these are?
   Remind the children about other seeds they may have sprouted. Corn kernels are seeds. They can grow into new corn plants with more ears of corn on them.

Plant Corn Seeds

Materials
loose corn kernels
plastic cup
paper towels

What to Do
1. "Plant" the unsprouted kernels in a clear plastic cup filled with damp paper towels, putting the seeds between the side of the cup and the towels so they are visible from outside the cup.

What to Talk About
1. Ask:
   - When do you think these will begin to grow?
   - What part do you think will/did grow first?

Many Varieties of Corn

Materials

variety of corn, including dried and fresh corn on the cob, ears of different colors and sizes, popcorn, and feed corn

What to Do

1. Varieties of corn can be found at farmers' markets, craft stores, feed stores, and groceries.
2. Pass around the varieties of corn and talk about their uses.
3. Ask the children what they notice about the varieties of corn.

What to Talk About

1. Big, little, different colors: it's all corn. Many people in the world eat corn and feed corn to their livestock animals. Corn can be made into many different foods.
2. Ask:
   - What kind of food made from corn is your favorite?
   - Has anyone ever grown corn or seen it growing anywhere?

The Story's Ending

Materials

Corn Is Maize by Aliki

What to Do

1. Finish telling the story of *Corn Is Maize* by Aliki.

What to Talk About

1. Today people all over the world eat corn. There are many kinds of corn.

Hold a Model of Our Earth, a Globe

Materials

globe of Earth

What to Do

1. Unveil the globe and remind the children that the globe is not a ball—no bouncing!
2. Put the globe in the center of the circle and see if they can relate it to the photo from the previous activity before you explain the relationship.
3. Show on the globe where corn originated (Mexico) and where it is grown now (all over the world).

What to Talk About

1. Ask:
   - What is this? (A model of the Earth. Just as toy cars are models of real cars, the globe is a model of the real earth.)
   - What shape is it?
   - Is there a photograph of it in this room?

A Photograph of the Earth

Materials
photograph of Earth, poster-size if available

What to Do
1. A photograph of the Earth can be found in many school supply stores and catalogues, in bookstores, or it can be ordered from *Sky and Telescope* magazine or The Astronomical Society of the Pacific.
2. Show the children the photograph of Earth.

What to Talk About
1. Ask:
   - What do you see in this photograph?
   - What is the blue color?
   - What is the white; the brown?
2. Ask the children to identify what they see (planet, ocean, clouds, land).

Corn Tastes Good

Materials
corn snacks

What to Do
1. Eat a corn snack, such as corn kernels cooked with a little butter and salt (great for small motor development as the children pick it up kernel by kernel), corn pudding, polenta, cornbread in its many forms, homemade corn tortillas, popcorn, or a prepared snack from the grocery.

What to Talk About
1. Yum, no wonder corn is grown around the world now!

Books to Read
Be Blest: A Celebration of the Seasons by Mary Beth Owens
Corn Is Maize: The Gift of the Indians by Aliki
The Earth Is Good: A Chant in Praise of Nature by Michael DeMunn
Looking Down by Steve Jenkins
Planet Earth/Inside Out by Gail Gibbons

Follow-Up Activities
- Continue observing the sprouting corn.
- Have the children draw and label the plant parts—the roots, the leaf, the stalk, and the nodes—as Aliki did in the book, *Corn Is Maize*.
- When the children talk about where their families are from or where they went for Thanksgiving (or any other trip), trace the path on the globe. For the rest of the year, whenever you read a book that specifies a certain location, find the story location on the globe.
- Cook something from corn!

Bringing Science Home!
A Note Home to Families About Corn and an Introduction to the Globe

Dear Families,

Do you remember the first time you ate corn? How many ways does your family prepare corn? We have been touching and exploring many kinds of corn, including dried corn (like popcorn) and fresh ears of corn. We put some dried kernels (seeds) into a cup to sprout, and we have been observing what has been happening.

Corn originated in Mexico but is now grown all over the world. The globe that is in our classroom is a model of our Earth, the world we live on. The children held a globe, and correctly called it a ball because it is round. We found where Mexico is located on the globe. The globe shows the water and the land, but a photograph of our Earth also shows the clouds above. It is such a beautiful home!

Winter Birds

OBJECTIVES
To introduce the common birds in your area
To notice nature's limited palette

SCIENCE TABLE
Put the following items on the Science Table: the bird shapes (see "To Get Ready") and found bird-related objects, such as feathers, eggshells (clean and dry), and nests (only if they have fallen from a tree because some nests are used more than one year). Keep these items out for a few weeks, or as long as you are exploring this experience with the children.

TO GET READY—

Exploring Winter Birds

Materials
cardboard, plastic, or art foam
marker
scissors
bird identification books or charts

What to Do
1. Comment on birds you see around the school and flying by the playground.
2. Name them or ask the children to name them, if possible. It's okay to use an appropriate made-up name, such as "the black ones with the white speckles" or the "red bird."

⚲ Each science experience has several activities, which, if done in sequence, build on each other.
Doing everything from "To Get Ready" to "Follow-Up Activities" will give children repeated opportunities to understand concepts.
The individual activities can be used separately, and children often want to repeat their favorite activities.

3. Ahead of time, make silhouette shapes of familiar local birds by tracing around the pictures in books or charts, then cutting the shapes from cardboard, plastic, or art foam.
4. Make them life sized, if possible, or keep them proportional to each other. Some common birds are crows, jays, chickadees, cardinals, starlings, gulls, sparrows, and pigeons.
5. Children can handle the shapes at the Science Table or use them to make crayon rubbings.

Bird Food

Materials
wire bird feeder for suet cakes
suet cakes
bird seed

What to Do
1. Put out a suet bird feeder, a suet cake, and a bag of a birdseed mixture for the children to handle and explore.

What to Talk About
1. Ask:
   - Where have you seen birds eating? (Different birds have different eating habits. They eat different foods and they eat in different places. Crows, pigeons, and cardinals prefer to eat seeds on a flat surface, such as the ground, and chickadees prefer to eat them higher up, and can hang onto a branch while eating. House sparrows will eat anywhere. Gulls grab food and fly away with it.)
2. Using the cutouts from the previous activity, show the children the shapes of the birds as you mention them.

Bird Shapes and Colors

Materials
bird identification chart or book

What to Do
1. Look at a bird identification book or chart and ask the children to point out pictures of the birds whose shapes they have handled or other birds they have seen.

What to Talk About
1. Ask:
   - Where should we put the food for each bird, so the bird will find it? (While they are deciding, ask the children to take note of the bird's size, and where they may have seen it eating.)
2. Point out the colors of the birds. Ask:
   - Are they all the same color?
   Explain that an artist shows other people what the birds look like in nature by using the colors of the actual birds.

Bird Shape Rubbings

Materials
familiar bird shapes (see page 74)
large crayons with the labels peeled off: black, red, blue, gray, and brown
paper
masking tape

What to Do
1. Using the bird shapes, make simple rubbings of the most common birds in your area, perhaps a crow, a pigeon, a cardinal, a jay, a chickadee, a house sparrow, and a gull.
2. Tape the bird shapes to the table, tape a piece of paper over the shape, and rub large crayons over the paper.

3. Have only the appropriate crayons available, such as black, gray, red, blue, and brown.

What to Talk About

1. Ask:
   - How is a crow different from a cardinal, and so on?
   - What size is your bird?
   - What shape is your bird's beak?
   - What color(s) does your bird have? (Explain that by using the actual colors of the birds in our rubbings we can show other people what the real birds look like. We could look for a long time and would never see a pink crow in nature! Scientists record what they see in nature. This does not mean that they should limit their creative artwork to nature's colors.)

Books to Read

Cardinal and Sunflowers by James Preller
Crinkleroot's 25 Birds Every Child Should Know by Jim Arnosky
Feathers for Lunch by Lois Ehlert
Have You Seen Birds? by Joanne F. Oppenheim
Our Yard Is Full of Birds by Anne Rockwell
Snowballs by Lois Ehlert
Urban Roosts: Where Birds Nest in the City by Barbara Bash
Any bird identification book

Follow-Up Activities

- Make the following bird feeders with the children. Let them take the feeders home or hang them outside the school.

  1. Tie string loops on pinecones. Smear peanut butter (or solid vegetable shortening) on the pinecones and then roll them in birdseed.

  2. Another good bird feeder can be made by brushing one side of a piece of bread with egg white (pasteurized egg whites in a carton are available in the dairy coolers of some grocery stores), and then pressing it in birdseed spread out in a pan (adults only). Put a piece of string through one edge and let the bread dry to rock-hardness before hanging it outside.

- Older children can record the birds they see on a graph. The bird sightings can be done over the period of a week on the playground or on a bird-watching walk around the neighborhood. Using the natural colors, each child makes a rubbing of the shape of the bird they saw and then cuts it out. The rubbings are taped to the graph (a large sheet of paper), each shape in its own column. The graph makes it easy to see how many of one kind of bird (crows, pigeons, sparrows, etc.) the children observed. Adding the bird names to the graph is optional.

Bringing Science Home!
A Note Home to Families About Winter Birds

Dear Families,

How many birds of different colors can you see in your neighborhood? We used those colors when we made rubbings of common bird shapes. As scientists, we record what we observe in nature. Your child may want to name the birds he or she sees. It's okay to use an appropriate made-up name such as "the black ones with the white speckles" or the "red bird."

It's also fun to look for your favorite bird in these books:

- *Crinkleroot's 25 Birds Every Child Should Know* by Jim Arnosky
- *Have You Seen Birds?* by Barbara Reid
- *Our Yard Is Full of Birds* by Anne Rockwell

What Is Melting?

TO GET READY—

Exploring Melting

Talk about the states of matter—liquid, solid, and gas—as the children go about their day.

- ♀ "I'm pouring some liquid juice into your cup. It's flowing."
- ♀ "Ouch! The block that dropped on my foot sure is a hard solid."
- ♀ "I can squish this playdough, but it does not flow. It doesn't feel wet. Is it a solid or a liquid?"

Use Body Heat to Melt Chocolate

Materials

balls of wax
chocolate chips

What to Do

1. Give each child a small ball of wax and a chocolate chip to hold in separate hands. If you give the children one chocolate chip to eat and one to hold, they will be more likely to hold the chip. Reassure the children that any time they get sticky hands they may wash them.

2. Jump up and down 20 times and march around the room twice (to get the children's hands hot enough to melt the chocolate chip).

OBJECTIVE
To learn that heating a solid can make a change called melting, a change in state

SCIENCE TABLE
Float an "iceberg" in the water table or a bucket of water. Make the iceberg by freezing a large plastic bag full of water (when the water is frozen, peel off the plastic bag). The water can be colored with food coloring. Small toys can be frozen within the water. When the ice is removed from the bag, it is an irregular iceberg shape. Keep making icebergs for a few weeks, or as long as you are exploring this experience with the children.

♀ Each science experience has several activities, which, if done in sequence, build on each other.
Doing everything from "To Get Ready" to "Follow-Up Activities" will give children repeated opportunities to understand concepts.
The individual activities can be used separately, and children often want to repeat their favorite activities.

🕯 Beeswax will melt more easily than paraffin and can be purchased from craft stores or beekeeper supply companies.

What to Talk About

1. Reassure the children that melting is good and not an undesirable mess.
2. Ask:
   🕯 Did any change happen to the wax or chocolate?
   🕯 Which is softer?
3. Have all the children open their hands to show the others. Some chips will be more melted than others.
4. Ask:
   🕯 What happened to your chocolate chip?
   🕯 What is melting? (Melting is a change in state of being from a solid to a liquid.)
   🕯 Did the wax melt in your hands?
   🕯 What else can melt?
   🕯 What else can change from a solid into a liquid?
5. Wash hands!

🕯 What makes ice melt?
🕯 What does it change to, what is the name of its new form? (Water, a liquid.)

Ice Melts

Materials
ice cubes
small paper cups
paper towels

What to Do

1. Give each child an ice cube in a small paper cup.
2. Encourage them to hold the ice cube, lick it, or crunch it, exploring its properties.

What to Talk About

1. Ask:
   🕯 Is the ice a solid (like a block), liquid (like something you drink), or a gas (like air)?
   🕯 What is happening to your ice cube?

Melt Wax

Materials
new birthday candles and melted ones
small bowl of wet sand
matches

What to Do

1. Ahead of time, tell the children that you will blow out the candle together. Warn them to stay back from the candle flame. Place a bowl of wet sand next to you.
2. Light a birthday candle, place it into the bowl of wet sand, and watch it melt. Blow it out when it has melted halfway. The children will probably want you to do it again.

3. Alternatively, let them handle an already partially melted candle with plenty of drips. **Note:** Closely supervise this activity.

What to Talk About

1. Ask:
   - What will happen to this candle if I light it?
   - How do you melt a candle?
   - Why does the wax drip? (It changes to a liquid.)
   - How hot would a rock have to be to melt?

Melted Rock

Materials
matches
volcanic rock

What to Do

1. Have the children handle volcanic rock that was melted at one time.
   - A volcanic rock called pumice can be purchased in the nail care aisle of a drugstore or from scientific supply companies.
2. Hold a match to the rock to try to melt it. **Note:** Closely supervise this activity.

What to Talk About

1. Ask:
   - How hot would a rock have to be to melt?
   - Which melts most easily: the chocolate chip, the wax, or the rock?
   - Which is hardest to melt?

Melt Chocolate Again!

Materials
chocolate chips
paper towels

What to Do

1. Repeat the chocolate chip melting—just for fun!

Books to Read
Once Upon Ice: And Other Frozen Poems selected by Jane Yolen
Solid, Liquid, or Gas? by Fay Robinson

Follow-Up Activities

- During outside time, take some ice cubes and a dish of water outside to see if the ice cubes or the water will change their states of being (melt/freeze).
- Paint with ice. Fill small paper cups halfway with water, put in a craft stick, and freeze. When the ice is solid, remove from the cups and use as a paintbrush. First sprinkle $\frac{1}{2}$ teaspoon of paint powder on the paper and then slide the ice over it to paint as the ice melts.
- Make Popsicles by freezing small cups of juice. Place a craft stick in each cup to use as the handle.

Bringing Science Home!
A Note Home to Families About Melting

Dear Families,

Children are amazed to see a solid change to a liquid. Melting ice is probably the most familiar experience your preschooler has with changing the state of a substance from solid to liquid. Our activities included trying to melt two other substances using the body heat of our hands—chocolate chips and wax. The chocolate chips melted easily but the balls of wax did not. Then, we watched while fire, something much hotter than our hands, melted the wax. We tried melting a rock with a match (the children observed while I held the match) but the fire wasn't hot enough.

What Can the Wind Do?

OBJECTIVES
To use air to move objects, imitating the wind
To raise the question of what makes the wind

SCIENCE TABLE
Put a collection of hand-held fans and cotton balls or packing peanuts on the Science Table. The fans can be made by folding a piece of paper back and forth into accordion folds. Gather the folds at one end and staple them together. Keep them out for a few weeks, or as long as you are exploring this experience with the children.

TO GET READY—
Exploring What the Wind Can Do

Notice the wind during outside time—its speed and what objects it can move. With the children, lie down on the ground or a blanket, looking up and devoting your full attention to the world above. If you do this first, the children will join in. It's easier to see the wind moving the clouds and branches when you are still. With older children, do a guided imagery version inside. Say, "Lie down on the floor and look up at the pretend sky. What do you see? Oh, there's a bird. No, it's a rocket ship! Now what do you see? Look at the clouds. They are moving." Four-year-olds will enthusiastically join in with their own, sometimes fantastic, sightings.

Each science experience has several activities, which, if done in sequence, build on each other.
Doing everything from "To Get Ready" to "Follow-Up Activities" will give children repeated opportunities to understand concepts.
The individual activities can be used separately, and children often want to repeat their favorite activities.

Blow It

Materials

cotton balls or packing peanuts

What to Do

1. Place a pretend cloud (cotton ball or packing peanut) in front of each child.
2. Ask the children to move it without touching it with their bodies. If no one thinks of it, show the children how to blow the "cloud" across the table.

What to Talk About

1. Ask:
   - How is your breath like the wind? (Both are moving air.)

Pretend to Be the Wind

Materials

Styrofoam, foam board, art foam, or other buoyant material
scissors or box cutter
shallow dish, such as a cake pan

What to Do

1. Cut foam board into small, boat hull shapes, such as a 2cm x 5cm rectangle with a point on each end.
2. Float these sailboats in an inch of water in a cake pan or other shallow dish.
3. Ask the children to move the boats using the air from their breath to be the wind.

What to Talk About

1. Ask:
   - What can the wind do? (Move sailboats, water, clouds, smells, seeds, balloons, kites, and birds.)
   The children will discover, to their joy, that a gale-force breath will capsize the boats.

Move Like a Windblown Object

What to Do

1. Act out the following riddle:

The Wind
Stand in a circle with plenty of room for each child to move and pretend to be blown by the wind:

What moves the clouds in the sky?
What stirs the leaves on the trees?
What waves the flag flying high?
What blows my kite back to me?
(Now turn to your neighbor and stage whisper)
It's the wind, the wind, the wind.

Wind Socks

Materials

plastic soda bottles
tissue paper in bright colors
glue sticks
markers or stickers
cloth ribbons or string
scissors

What to Do

1. Slice the middle section of any size plastic soda bottles into 1-inch wide hoops (you can usually cut three or four hoops from one bottle), one for each windsock, and recycle the top and bottom. This will be the "mouth" of the windsock.

Wind Ribbons

Materials
cloth ribbons
plastic curtain loops
scissors

1. Cut three 20-inch lengths of brightly colored cloth ribbon, using a variety of colors.
2. Loop them through a plastic curtain ring with a half-hitch knot to complete the wind ribbon.
3. Watch the ribbons move as you dance holding the ring!

Books to Read
Gilberto and the Wind by Marie Hall Ets
Let's Try It Out in the Air: Hands-On Early-Learning Science Activities by Seymour Simon and Nicole Fauteux

Follow-Up Activities
⚘ Give each child a straw and a fluffy feather. Insert the feather into the end of the straw and blow the feather out!
⚘ Fly a kite.

2. Fold a sheet of tissue paper into a rectangle.
3. Have the children draw on it or decorate it with stickers.
4. Then help them glue just the long edges (opposite the fold) together using glue sticks.
5. Ask the children to put glue on the plastic soda bottle hoop, and then help them put one end of the tissue paper around the tube to make the "mouth" of the windsock.
6. Using a hole punch, punch two holes through the plastic hoop to attach a string or ribbon for a handle. If you wish, cut the end of the tissue paper tube into fringes that will flutter in the wind.

Bringing Science Home!
A Note Home to Families About What Wind Can Do

Dear Families,

Seeing is often believing with preschoolers. We can't see the wind but we can help our children wonder about it by noticing aloud when we see the results of the wind's actions. Look at the tree branches moving around. Do you see the clouds moving in the sky? Will the wind hold up the kite? The wind, as an everyday experience, is thankfully not often as dramatic as a tornado. But many scientists began important work when they wondered about everyday experiences that everyone else always took for granted. We do important work when we encourage our children to ask questions even if we don't have all the answers. If your child feels that asking questions is proper behavior for children, then the answers will follow.

Planting Peas on Presidents' Day

(Or earlier or later depending on when spring comes in your geographic area)

OBJECTIVES
To notice and be part of the first stirring of spring
To plant seeds as early as possible for your geographic area
To observe seeds sprouting, growing, and producing fruit

Peas are one of the few vegetables that can be planted outside and bear fruit before the school year ends.

SCIENCE TABLE
Put indoor-planted pea seeds and garden catalogues that the children can cut up to make signs for their growing peas on the Science Table. Keep them out for a few weeks, or as long as you are exploring this experience with the children.

TO GET READY—
Exploring Planting

Talk about the beginning signs of spring: longer days, occasionally warmer weather, leaves and buds of spring-flowering bulbs growing, and early flowering bushes, such as forsythia, Japanese quince, and pussy willow.

Preparing the Peas for Planting

Materials

pea seeds (the edible-pod varieties with the shortest time to maturity and those needing little support for growing are best)
container

What to Do

1. Most seeds are treated with insecticides to keep them from being eaten before they are planted, so be sure to wash them gently beforehand. Warn the children not to put them in their mouths and to wash their hands after handling.
   Note: Supervise this activity closely.

🍐 Each science experience has several activities, which, if done in sequence, build on each other.
Doing everything from "To Get Ready" to "Follow-Up Activities" will give children repeated opportunities to understand concepts.
The individual activities can, of course, be used separately, and children often want to repeat their favorite activities.

2. For planting either inside or outside, have the children soak pea seeds in a dish of water for 2-5 hours. They can be kept moist up to 24 hours without turning to mush if you drain off most of the water and cover the seeds before leaving school that day.

Planting Inside

Materials

pea seeds (the edible-pod varieties with the shortest time to maturity and those needing little support for growing are best)
clear plastic container
zipper-closure plastic bags
paper towels

What to Do

1. Begin this activity a week ahead of outdoor planting so the children can see the sprouting seed. (The peas that grow indoors will not survive to maturity without special care, so to see plants produce pea pods, be sure to plant more seeds outside.)
2. "Plant" a few seeds in a single clear plastic container for the classroom or prepare individual zipper-closure plastic bags so each child has a few seeds of his or her own.
3. Fill the container with paper towels and have the children "plant" the peas in between the towels and the sides of the container so any growth will be visible. Or, put one folded paper towel in each bag and the pea seeds on top of the towel.
4. Add enough water to just soak the paper towel, and then close the container/bag.

What to Talk About

1. Ask:
    - Do you think these seeds will grow?
    - What do they need to grow?
    - What will happen first?
    - What will they grow to be?

Measure the Growth

Materials

pea seeds in containers or bags (from the previous activity)

What to Do

1. Note and measure the growth of the root and sprout during circle time or when children arrive in the morning. Make it part of the morning routine, so that the peas aren't forgotten.
2. Relative measuring is appropriate. "The root is shorter than the seed/my fingernail/my braid. The sprout has lots of/hardly any leaves."
3. The key to keeping the peas alive is to keep the towel damp but not allow water to pool in the container/bag. Water it a tiny bit

every week. (This can be a child's job. Help him or her add just one teaspoon of water or two squirts with a spray mist bottle.) Also keep the sprouts cool (off radiators and windowsills).

4. For better viewing, tape the bags to a wall.

Planting Outside

Materials

pea seeds (the edible-pod varieties with the shortest time to maturity and those needing little support for growing are best)
an outside garden area or a large pot
digging tools (soup spoons sold at thrift stores are just the right size for preschoolers)

What to Do

1. Have the children plant garden peas in an outdoor garden area, such as a large pot, a small spot next to a bush, or a designated garden plot, where it receives at least 4 hours of daylight (no shadows) a day.

2. Loosen the dirt with a shovel or garden fork to make planting and growing easier.

3. Enrich the dirt with compost or leaf mulch, if available, or commercial compost. The pea seeds should be pre-soaked 2-5 hours.

4. Plant the pre-soaked seeds about one inch deep (for the children, one pinky finger deep). Don't worry if subsequent gardeners unearth someone else's peas, they can just be stuck back in!

What to Talk About

1. Ask:
   - How do we know that it is safe to plant peas now, that they won't freeze but will be able to grow?
   - What signs of spring have we seen? (Tree buds swelling, trees flowering, leaves and buds of spring-flowering bulbs growing above ground, longer days. Peas can be planted as soon as the ground is clear of snow and thawed enough to dig.)
   - Do you think the seeds will grow?
   - What do they need to grow?
   - What will they grow to be? (For everything there is a season. Peas grow

best in cool weather, now, before it gets
hot in the summer. If the seed has what
it needs, it will sprout. It needs some
water and a little warmth.)

Books to Read

Inch by Inch: The Garden Song by David Mallett, et al
The Ugly Vegetables by Grace Lin

Follow-Up Activities

- Plant peas inside if you haven't already.
- Measure, draw, or chart the root and sprout
  growth.
- Watch the ground for sprouting pea plants.
  Count the number of days until they show
  above ground.
- Serve a snack of snow peas.
- Sing a song: A traditional call-and-response
  song, such as "John the Rabbit" or "Ol' John
  Rabbit," versions of which can be heard on
  Mike and Peggy Seeger's *American Folksongs
  for Children* or Sharon, Lois and Bram's *Mainly
  Mother Goose*:

Oh, John the rabbit	*yes, ma'am*
Had a mighty bad habit	*yes, ma'am*
Of jumpin' in my garden	*yes, ma'am*
And eating my peas	*yes, ma'am*
He ate my tomatoes	*yes, ma'am*
And my sweet potatoes	*yes, ma'am*
And if I live	*yes, ma'am*
To see next fall	*yes, ma'am*
Maybe I won't	*yes, ma'am*
Garden at all!	*yes, ma'am!*

Bringing Science Home!
A Note Home to Families About Planting Peas on Presidents' Day

Dear Families,

It's hard to believe that the year is turning to spring! Like our children's growth, the change seems imperceptible unless we measure it somehow. The children are doing just that by planting pea seeds, some outside in the dirt to grow and bear fruit before the school year ends, and some inside in a plastic bag, to observe the seeds sprouting. We are wondering what will happen first. Will a root or leaf grow first?

Peas are one of the few vegetables that can be planted outside at this time of year. We will measure their growth by comparing the plant height to our fingers. What will the weather be like when the pea plants are as tall as our hands? And what will it be like when the plants flower and when the peas grow big enough to eat?

Waiting for Mantises to Hatch

TO GET READY—
Exploring Mantises

1. Learn the following insect poem:

   Bigger Than You
   Crawling, crawling on my skin,
   Little insect, I know we're not kin.
   You have six legs, I have two,
   Yet little insect, I am bigger than you!

2. Provide some of the suggested books (see page 96) about a variety of insects for the children to look at.

Mantis Puppet

Materials
picture of a mantis
marker
copy machine
stiff plastic, cardboard, or art foam
scissors
tape
brass paper fasteners

What to Do

1. To make the puppet, trace a picture of a mantis that clearly shows the head, body, and legs.
2. Enlarge the drawing on a copy machine so that the puppet will be larger than in real life (and easier for the children to handle). The larger size makes it less fragile and more easily seen.

Each science experience has several activities, which, if done in sequence, build on each other.
Doing everything from "To Get Ready" to "Follow-Up Activities" will give children repeated opportunities to understand concepts.
The individual activities can be used separately, and children often want to repeat their favorite activities.

3. Make the puppet from stiff plastic, cardboard, or art foam, cutting out each leg separately.
4. Reinforce the material with tape where you hinge the pieces together.
5. Hinge it at the joints with brass paper fasteners. Include all six legs even though it's a flat puppet.

Introducing the Insect

Materials
mantis puppet (see previous activity)

What to Do
1. To introduce the mantis puppet, make it move and talk, saying to each child, "Hello, my name is Mantis. What is your name?"
2. Make sure each child has a chance to interact with the puppet.

What to Talk About
1. Ask:
   - ♀ How many legs do you have?
   - ♀ How many legs does the mantis have? (Body parts of insects do not correspond one to one with our body parts.)

Compare Human Bodies to Insect Bodies

Materials
mantis puppet
insect identification book

What to Do
1. Ask the children to count the number of legs on the mantis puppet (there should be six).
2. Make the puppet catch an "insect" (first catch your hand creeping across the table, then catch any willing child's hand) using the puppet's front legs. (Many children love to "be chased" as long as they know they are safe.)
3. Look for a mantis in the insect identification book.

What to Talk About
1. Ask:
   - ♀ What other parts of this insect can you name?
   - ♀ Do we have these on our heads? (antenna)
   - ♀ What does its mouth look like? Look for photos that show the mouth parts, called palps.

Body Play

Materials

none needed

What to Do

1. Sing the following to the tune of "Head, Shoulders, Knees and Toes" and gesture to the pretend body part:

   Head, thorax, ab-do-men, abdomen. (The insect's thorax is the part where the limbs are attached—point to your chest. The insect's abdomen is the part after the legs are attached—point to your bottom.)
   Head, thorax, ab-do-men, abdomen.
   Eyes, antenna, and mouth and palps, (Point to your mouth, then make your index fingers into tiny arms at your mouth to be the palps, which are mouth parts.)
   Head, thorax, ab-do-men, abdomen.

Baby Mantises

Materials

mantis egg case (use an empty egg case left over from last year or order a new one from a biological supply company)

What to Do

1. Order the mantis egg case from a biological company (see resource lists on page 232).
2. With great drama tell a story about the mother mantis laying her eggs (see next column).
3. Find a photograph of a mantis laying eggs to use as a prop.
4. Show the mantis' egg case and ask the children to touch it with just one finger. (Once the egg case has hatched, the children can handle it more thoroughly and even cut it open.)

   Once upon a time the mother mantis got ready to lay her eggs. She squeezed some foam out of her body onto a branch. Then she squeezed her eggs out of her body and into the foam. The foam got hard and the eggs were safe inside. Whether it rained or snowed, the eggs stayed dry inside the foam while the baby mantises grew and got ready to hatch.

What to Talk About

1. Ask:
   - When do you think the insects will hatch?
   - What will the hatchlings look like?
   - How many babies will there be?
   Let's draw a picture of what we think they might look like. The children may have some concerns about where the mother is during this time. They will accept it when you tell them that many animal babies do not need to be taken care of by a parent when they hatch because are ready to take care of themselves.

Preparing a Mantis Home

Materials

large plastic container, such as a soda bottle, a pretzel tub, or an aquarium
scissors
craft foam
cardboard, if necessary
mantis egg case (use an empty egg case left over from last year or order a new one from a biological supply company)
branch to hold the egg case
food source for mantis

What to Do

1. Make a mantis habitat, a safe place for the eggs to hatch. A large plastic container such as a two-liter soda bottle, a pretzel tub, or an aquarium works well.

2. Cut a circular hole in the side of the container that can be filled with a circle of craft foam for the stopper and/or make a lid of foam.

3. If the aquarium does not have a close-fitting lid, fashion one from cardboard with an access hole. The foam allows air in and keeps the insects from going out. (Baby mantises can get out through small openings and will die in the classroom.)

4. Tie the egg case to a branch and put it in the habitat.
   Note: Make preparations for a food source such as fruit flies if you intend to keep any of the mantises for observation after hatching. The food insects can be ordered from the same supplier as the egg cases.

What to Talk About

1. Ask:
   - Will the mantises be big or small when they hatch?
   - What do they eat?

Observing Growing and Changing

Materials

egg cases and habitat from previous activities

What to Do

1. Keep the mantis egg cases in the classroom.
2. Monitor the container for hatching "babies," which may take as long as three weeks.
3. When the mantises hatch they can be released outside the same day or kept in the classroom for several days, even several weeks if you provide food and mist the

inside wall of the habitat once a day. (They will begin to eat each other if no other food is provided.)

What to Talk About

1. Ask:
   - What do the insects look like at different stages in their lives—as babies, as "teenagers," and as adults? (If the children have observed the growth and change of a caterpillar into a butterfly, review the "growing up" of a butterfly. It started as a caterpillar; a different shape when it hatched from its egg than the adult butterfly that laid the egg.)
   - What do these baby mantises look like?
   - Do you think they will make chrysalis and metamorphose into another shape or just stay the same shape and get bigger? (They will stay the same shape as they grow and molt their skin.)
   - What do their mouths and mouth parts look like?
   - What do they eat? (These mantises eat other insects.) Show the fruit fly culture.
   - What might eat the mantis? (Birds.)

Books to Read

Backyard Hunter: The Praying Mantis by Bianca Lavies

Bugs! Bugs! Bugs! by Bob Barner

Creepy Crawlies and the Scientific Method: More Than 100 Hands-on Science Experiments for Children by Sally Kneidel

How to Hide a Butterfly and Other Insects by Ruth Heller

A book with clear illustrations of various animals metamorphosing as they grow is *Mealworms: Raise Them, Watch Them, See Them Change* by Adrienne Mason

For excellent information on setting up small-animal habitats and maintaining them, read:

Pet Bugs: A Kid's Guide to Catching and Keeping Touchable Insects and *Creepy Crawlies and the Scientific Method: More Than 100 Hand-On Science Experiments for Children* both by Sally Stenhouse Kneidel

Bringing Science Home!
A Note Home to Families About Waiting for Mantises to Hatch

Dear Families,

How many insects are there in the world? Most will say that there are too many. It seems like they are always where we don't want them to be. But these small animals fascinate children. Children love to observe ants, butterflies, and caterpillars as they play. And even children who don't like creepy crawlies on the loose want to see them in their classroom cage or habitat.

Mantis egg cases have arrived in the classroom. These egg cases are formed by the female mantis in the fall and are tough enough to survive the winter. The praying mantis is the most familiar species of this group of insects.

We have been wondering when they will hatch. The children's guesses about how many babies will hatch from the egg case range from 1 to 100! Will the baby mantises be caterpillars like the baby butterflies? That is another question the children will answer in time. The class will do some research to find out what to feed the baby mantises and how to care for them.

A Tree Is Nice

TO GET READY—

Exploring Trees

Materials

tree
blanket
large crayons, with the paper peeled off
paper
tree identification book

OBJECTIVE
To use our senses to experience a tree while learning about the life cycle of tree plants

SCIENCE TABLE
Put a variety of the parts of a tree, such as slices through a tree trunk, leaves, bark, and twigs, on your Science Table. Keep the items out for a few weeks or for as long as you are exploring this experience with the children.

What to Do

1. First, go hug a tree. Feel the bark and smell it. The children may never have been so close to a tree, especially in urban areas where trees are routinely trimmed of all their lower branches to prevent climbing.

2. Ask:
   - How is the tree attached to the ground?
   - Did someone stick the trunk into the ground?
   - Did it pop up already grown?

3. Spread a blanket and lie down under the tree and look up at the branches.

Each science experience has several activities, which, if done in sequence, build on each other.
Doing everything from "To Get Ready" to "Follow-Up Activities" will give children repeated opportunities to understand concepts.
The individual activities can be used separately, and children often want to repeat their favorite activities.

Where Do Trees Come From?

Materials

tree seeds (such as acorns, pinecones, apple, peach, orange, or mango seeds or maple tree seed "helicopters")

What to Do

1. Begin with a discussion of where trees come from.
2. Most children will know that they grow in the ground.
3. Pass around tree seeds for the children to handle and explore.

What to Talk About

1. Ask:
   - How do trees get started growing?
   - What size was the smallest tree you ever saw?
   - How small is a tree when it is a baby?

Hold a Baby Tree

Materials

tree seedlings with only two to six leaves

What to Do

1. Pass around some tree seedlings, just a few inches tall with only two to six leaves. (You can sprout these yourself or dig up some in the spring from your own yard, in between cracks in the sidewalk, or from a wooded area. Never take a plant from a protected park, but removing one of the tree seedlings that sprout in the bits of woods between homes or alongside parking lots is fine because most of them will never survive to be even a young tree. It's okay to dig them up and maybe some of the children will be able to give them a home.)

4. Help the children make a tree bark rubbing by holding a piece of paper against the trunk while a child rubs a crayon (held sideways) over the page to reveal the texture of the bark.
5. Bring some leaves back to the classroom to make more rubbings. Look up the name of your tree in a tree identification book. (See Stretch Your Senses, page 51, about befriending a special tree.)

What to Talk About

1. Ask:
   - Which is taller, you or the baby tree?
   - How many hands tall are you?
   - Is the baby tree even a hand tall yet?
   - How long do you think it would take for this tree to grow as big as the one outside?

Make a Leaf Rubbing

Materials
leaves
tape
paper
large crayons, with paper peeled off

What to Do

1. Tape a leaf to the table, tape a piece of paper over it and, holding a crayon sideways, rub back and forth until the leaf shape is revealed.
2. Using more than one color crayon will make an especially dramatic rubbing. (Children like to be surprised! If you can cover the leaves with the paper before the children see them they will enjoy seeing the unknown shape revealed as they rub.)

What to Talk About

1. Ask:
   - Could this tiny plant be a tree?
   - Have you ever seen a tree this small?

How Big?

Materials
ruler or class measuring hands (see page 226)

What to Do

1. This is a good time to measure some trees in the schoolyard or neighborhood, either with the class measuring hands (see page 226) or a ruler.

What to Talk About

1. Ask:
   - ？ What do you see in your rubbing?
   - ？ Is the leaf shape rounded or pointy?

The children may ask you for the type of tree their leaf came from. Depending on your knowledge or the amount of time you have to research, you can use general names such as "maple" or even made-up names such as "the pointy leaf tree."

A Tree Poem

Materials

Maples in the Mist by Minfong Ho, optional
Old Elm Speaks: Tree Poems by Kristine O'Connell
George

What to Do

1. Learn a poem about a tree.

   Baby Tree
   A baby tree that's just beginning,
   Is no more than a sprout.
   It has no trunk or branches,
   Just a stem with two leaves coming out.

Or look in *Maples in the Mist* by Minfong Ho for the poem "Little Pine" by Wang Jian, a Chinese poet of the Tang Dynasty, who lived from 766 to 830 AD.

Books to Read

Are Trees Alive? by Debbie S. Miller
Autumn Leaves by Ken Robbins
I Am a Leaf by Jean Marzollo
A Log's Life by Wendy Pfeffer
*Maples in the Mist: Poems for Children from the
        Tang Dynasty* by Minfong Ho
Meeting Trees by Scott Russell Sanders
Oak Tree by Paul Fleisher
Old Elm Speaks: Tree Poems by Kristine O'Connell
        George
A Tree Is Growing by Arthur Dorros
A Tree Is Nice by Janice May Udry

Follow-Up Activity

- ？ Plant one of the seedlings in a pot and care for it in the classroom or schoolyard.

Bringing Science Home!
A Note Home to Families About Trees

Dear Families,

A tree is nice, as the title of Janice May Udry's classic children's book says. Nice to see the strong trunk, and nice to see the spreading branches, especially if you lie on the ground and look up. A big tree with smooth or rough bark is nice to touch, and its leaves are cool and flat. The sound of leaves being moved by the wind is soothing. When we get close enough to smell the tree trunk we sometimes see small animals, like ants, which travel up and down the trunk.

All these small sensory experiences added together make a big impact on our environment. Shade-providing deciduous trees can save 10 to 50 percent on a home's summer cooling costs. One acre of trees produces enough oxygen every year for 1,000 people. Trees reduce flooding and erosion by catching rain on their leaves and branches and absorbing water through their roots.

How small is a baby tree? These wee ones are often over-looked so we brought some into the classroom to find out. Ask your child to tell you about them.

Dirt, What Is It?

OBJECTIVES
To look at, touch, and smell a sample of real soil and notice that it is a mixture of different-size particles
To see the tiny animals that live in dirt

SCIENCE TABLE
Put plastic jars or bags filled with soil samples from different locations (by the sandbox, from the teacher's yard, from the woods, and so on) on the Science Table. Having a variety of samples will give the children the chance to notice differences in soil composition. Maybe they would like to bring in some dirt from near their home. Also display two jars of soil samples mixed with water. The longer the sample sits still the more it will separate, so make one sample immobile by taping it to the table, and leave the other free for additional shaking. Keep these out for a few weeks, or as long as you are exploring this experience with the children.

TO GET READY—
Exploring Dirt
With the children, dig for worms and look for other tiny creatures in the dirt (soil) around the school. Such animals are more likely to live where there are dead leaves or wood for them to eat and hide under. Ask the children how many words they know that mean the same as "soil."

Use the Senses to Learn About Soil

Materials
1 quart of soil

What to Do
1. Take soil from a location where there will be some variety to it; that is, where the topsoil looks different from the soil underneath. Do not use well-cultivated garden soil or commercial topsoil. These are just too

---

🔎 Each science experience has several activities, which, if done in sequence, build on each other.
Doing everything from "To Get Ready" to "Follow-Up Activities" will give children repeated opportunities to understand concepts.
The individual activities can be used separately, and children often want to repeat their favorite activities.

homogenous to provide much information. Keep any insects or other small animals that are in the soil in your sample so the children can see them.

2. Encourage the children to look at, feel, and smell a soil sample dug from outside the school. Put the soil sample out on newspaper to make it easy to see and easy to clean up.

What to Talk About

1. Ask:
   - What questions could we ask about this soil? (Soil is a word for dirt or earth.)
   - How could we answer those questions?
   - Can you identify anything in the soil? List the parts of the soil named by the children. (mulch, roots, insects, tiny animals, sticks, stones, grass, sand, clay, mud, and so on).
   - Ask the children to give descriptive names to the soil sample (loose, sticky, smelly, sandy, clay-like, full of sticks, light brown, and dark brown).
   - Is it wet or dry?

Separate Soil Into Its Parts, Add Water...

Materials

plastic jars with lids
soil
water

What to Do

1. Take the soil from a location where there is some variety to it; that is, where the topsoil looks different from the soil underneath. Do not use well-cultivated garden soil or commercial topsoil. These are just too homogenous to provide much information.

2. Put one cup of soil into each plastic jar. Pour one cup of water into the jar. Have each child do this if you have enough jars.

What to Talk About

1. Ask:
   - What do you predict will happen when we pour the water in?
   - Will the water stay on top of the dirt? (The water goes into the spaces in the dirt; it does not stay on top. Bits of leaves or sticks may float.)

...And Shake

Materials

plastic jars filled with soil and water from previous activity

What to Do

1. Put the lids on the jars and take turns shaking them.

2. Encourage the children to watch the jar closely when they stop shaking it, so they can see the soil settling.

3. When the children are finished shaking, put the jars on a shelf where they won't be moved. Check them again after a few minutes for further settling.

What to Talk About

1. Ask:
   - What do you see happening?
   - Is the soil getting mixed up?
   - What will happen when we stop shaking?
   - Will the pieces in the water settle and go to the bottom, or stay suspended, floating in the water? (Notice that as the shaken dirt settles, it separates into layers, coarse pieces on the bottom grading into fine pieces at the top, with some leaves floating on the surface.)

Try to Make Dirt

Materials
soil
sand
wet clay or mud
pebbles
leaves and sticks (mulch works well)
plastic jars with lids or resealable plastic bags

What to Do

1. Have the children put a scoop of each material—clay, mud, sand, pebbles, or leaves and sticks—into a jar or bag. Also let the children come up with their own ideas of what they think goes into making dirt.

2. Add enough water to make one cup.

3. Put the lid on the jar or tape the bag closed and shake.

What to Talk About

1. Say, "We separated a soil sample. Now let's see if we can put one together."

2. Ask:
   - What do we need? (sand, mud, clay, dirt, leaves, and sticks)
   - What happens during the shaking? How do you think it will look after we stop shaking?

Is it Dirt Yet?

Materials
mixture from previous activity
soil from the school yard

What to Do

1. Pour out the "soil" the children just mixed next to the real soil sample from the schoolyard.

What to Talk About

1. Ask:

    ⸙ How does it look compared to the real soil sample made by natural processes? (In nature, soil is made over a long time, weeks and months and years. Water and the tiny animals in the soil, like earthworms, help break up the big chunks of rock and plant matter to make soil. They also help mix it together.)

    ⸙ How can we change this mixture into soil? The children may want to put the mixture back in the jar/bag, add water, and shake. The jars/bags of "made soil" can be kept on the Science Table. Some children like to add a descriptive label.

Check the Separated Soil Sample for Settling

Materials

jars of soil from "…And Shake"
paper
crayons or markers

What to Do

1. Look at the soil samples from "…And Shake" (page 104) again. Note how they have separated even more.

2. Ask any interested child to record the amount of separation by drawing it now and again a day or two. Not all children will want to do this. That's okay, some of them may observe the separation intently on later occasions.

What to Talk About

1. Invite the children to describe and name the layers of the separated soil sample (stones, pieces of dirt, sand, mud, muddy water, pieces of leaves and sticks). The children will probably note color differences before they see differences in grain size.

Books to Read

Compost Critters by Bianca Lavies
The Piggy in the Puddle by Charlotte Pomerantz (This book may help some children relax about handling dirt.)

Follow-Up Activities

⸙ For the rest of the week, look at the soil sample settling in the jar. Consider the following:

    ⸙ Do you see any layering?

    ⸙ What size pieces are on the bottom? What size pieces are next?

    ⸙ Is the water clear?

    ⸙ Do you want to record the separation by drawing pictures? (This will help the children notice the layers, like stripes.)

Bringing Science Home!
A Note Home to Families About Dirt—What Is It?

Dear Families,

We are encouraging your children to play in the dirt! As we are exploring the composition of dirt, we encourage you to dress your child in play clothes. Getting dirty should not be a concern at school because getting involved with the materials is part of learning.

Some children love to dig in the dirt with their hands and others prefer to work with a tool. Children used both styles of examining the dirt (or soil); they looked at, touched, and smelled a sample of real soil. Ask your child what he or she thought the soil smelled like.

As we looked closely, we found out that soil is a mixture of different size pieces of mud, sand, and sometimes stones or roots or little animals, such as earthworms. The children mixed some of these ingredients together to make some soil but found that it didn't look like the real thing.

Butterflies Change as They Grow

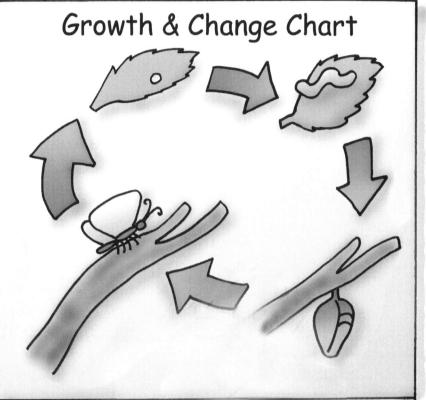

Growth & Change Chart

OBJECTIVES

To observe the life stages of a butterfly, from egg to caterpillar, to chrysalis, to adult butterfly

To observe the growth and change in an insect as it matures to adulthood and undergoes complete metamorphosis

SCIENCE TABLE

Put the butterfly habitat (see next page) and Growth and Change Chart on your Science Table. Keep it out for a few weeks, or as long as you are exploring this experience with the children.

Each science experience has several activities, which, if done in sequence, build on each other.
Doing everything from "To Get Ready" to "Follow-Up Activities" will give children repeated opportunities to understand concepts.
The individual activities can be used separately, and children often want to repeat their favorite activities.

The activities that make up this experience can be done with butterfly larvae (caterpillars) purchased from a biological supply company, or with Cabbage White butterflies (or other species) that you catch yourself. Raising the Cabbage White butterflies from the eggs takes longer but is less expensive than purchasing caterpillars.

Use an identification book to familiarize yourself with Cabbage White butterflies or another common but not endangered species. Cabbage Whites are yellowish white with a black dot and edging on the forewing. To have a good chance of getting both females and males, catch three butterflies to put in the habitat. A butterfly net is the easiest way to catch them. Make your own net with a three-foot tube of netting sewn to a wire coat hanger circle about one foot in diameter.

TO GET READY—
Exploring Butterflies

Materials
Caterpillars or Cabbage White butterflies (pieris rapae)
large plastic jar or container, or aquarium
open-celled foam or cheesecloth
broccoli or cabbage seedling
empty yogurt container
flowers
small plastic container, such as a film canister
sugar
cotton balls
plastic jar lid

What to Do
1. Either purchase caterpillars (such as Painted Lady butterfly larvae) or with the children's help, prepare a habitat for the butterflies you will catch. If you wish, follow the supplier's directions to keep the purchased larvae in the same container in which they arrive.

2. A large plastic container, such as one that pretzels come in, works well. Cut a circle of open-celled foam (such as foam used in cushions) to fit the opening to allow the passage of air, or cover the opening with cheesecloth. An aquarium with a fine screen cover is another good habitat container. Or cut window holes into a large cardboard box, and cover the holes with netting.

3. The butterflies will need a broccoli or cabbage seedling to lay eggs on. This can be purchased from a garden center and put into a yogurt cup to keep water from draining all over the floor of the habitat. Wash the seedling to get rid of any pesticides that may have been sprayed on it.

4. Put unsprayed flowers from your garden, (not the florist) into a small plastic container, such as a film canister, filled with water. Dandelions are fine.

5. Make a sugar solution by boiling 4 tablespoons water with 1 tablespoon sugar. Keep the solution refrigerated until used.

6. Pour the sugar-water solution onto a cotton ball and place on a plastic jar lid.

7. Add a few branches to the habitat for the butterflies to climb or land on.

8. Mist a tiny bit of fresh water on the inside wall of the habitat once a day for drinking.

9. Water the seedling occasionally to keep soil damp but not soaking.

10. Say and act out the following poem:

> **Butterfly**
> *Butterfly flitting from flower to flower,*
> *Drinking the nectar for hours and hours,*
> *Laying your egg under a leaf,*
> *When the night comes you go fast asleep.*
>
> *Caterpillar crawling along a green leaf,*
> *Munching the salad under your feet,*
> *Forming your chrysalis under a leaf,*
> *When the night comes you go fast asleep.*

11. Begin a discussion about favorite foods, perhaps at snack time or lunchtime.

12. Tell the children that your parents used to eat certain foods, and that you never liked them as a child but now you really do. They will have their own stories.

13. This lays the groundwork for understanding that the young and adult butterflies are very different and they like to eat different kinds of food. The mouthparts of the Painted Lady in adult form (butterfly) are specially shaped to be able to drink the nectar (flower juice) from particular plants. Their babies eat the leaves of their favorite plants.

Look at Butterflies and Caterpillars While Using Identification Books

Materials
butterflies or caterpillars
insect identification books
magnifying glasses

What to Do

1. Introduce the class to the Cabbage White butterflies or purchased caterpillars. Help the children look for them and the variety within this family of insects in insect identification books.

2. Get several books from the library or families at the school so children don't have to wait very long for their turn.

3. Use magnifying glasses to notice the eyes, hairs, and feet on the actual animals and in the illustrations.

What to Talk About

1. Ask:
   - What are these animals? (A caterpillar is the baby of a butterfly; it is called the larvae.)
   The children may wonder how the baby butterflies will survive without parental care. Reassure them that, unlike humans, many animals do not need their parents to grow up.
   - Let's look for them in an insect identification book. (There are many kinds of butterflies.)
   - What parts do they have to their bodies? (Refer to the identification books. Some children may want to point to the parts of the insect and have you read the name.)
   - Will they always be caterpillars?
   - What do they eat? (If you purchased the

larvae from a supply house they will come in a plastic cup with all the food they need in the form of a gray mash at the bottom of the cup. This food is similar to the food astronauts eat when they are in space; it is all ready to eat, lasts for a long time without spoiling, and isn't messy.)

- How can you tell they are eating? (Their mouthparts may be too small to see but the poop they produce is not.)
- What do their babies look like?
- Do they lay eggs?

Pretend Butterfly Tongues

Materials
party blowers

What to Do
1. Give each child a party blower, the kind that unrolls like a butterfly tongue when you blow into the end of it.

2. Form a pretend flower by holding your hand so that the fingertips touch the tip of your thumb to make an "O". (To make a more elaborate "flower", have the children decorate a cardboard tube with paper petals.)
3. Encourage the children to sip nectar from their flower by unrolling the blower/tongue and sticking it into the flower.

What to Talk About
1. Ask:
   - How long is your own tongue? (The party blowers are pretend butterfly tongues. A butterfly tongue is called a proboscis.)
   - What do you think butterflies eat? (You may want to wait until the children have had an opportunity to see a butterfly unroll its tongue and drink from a flower instead of telling them about it.)

Ongoing Observation of the Butterflies

Materials
Cabbage White butterflies
cotton balls
plastic jar lid
sugar solution
paper
crayons or markers

What to Do
1. Observe the Cabbage Whites (see page 109).
2. Perhaps the children would like to add butterfly duties to the job list. They can feed them by brushing a little bit of the sugar solution onto the flowers in the habitat.
3. The sugar solution can also be offered in a small feeder. Soak a cotton ball in the sugar

solution and put it on a lid in the habitat. Each day, change the cotton ball soaked in sugar solution.

4. Lightly mist a spot on the inside wall of the habitat daily with water.

5. The children may want to record their observations by drawing pictures or dictating to an adult.

What to Talk About

1. Ask:
   - What are the butterflies doing?
   - Where do they land?
   - Are they eating?
   - What are they eating?
   - Are they laying eggs?

Checking the Butterfly Habitat for Eggs

Materials

Cabbage White butterflies (Pieris rapae) in their habitat
poster board
markers

What to Do

1. Look to see if eggs are laid on the underside of the seedling's leaves. They are about 1 millimeter long, yellow, and laid singly.

2. If they have laid eggs, the butterflies may not live much longer.

What to Talk About

1. Say, "If we touch this egg we might squash it. Butterfly eggs do not have a shell like chicken eggs."

2. Ask:
   - When do you think it will hatch?
   - What do you think the baby will look like?

Have the Caterpillars Hatched?

Materials

Cabbage White butterfliles (Pieris rapae) in their habitat

What to Do

1. Check the eggs daily to see if they have hatched. The tiny caterpillars will be just a little longer than the egg and the same color as the leaf. They are hard to see!

2. Look for tiny new holes in the leaves as a clue that a newly hatched caterpillar is eating it.

What to Talk About

1. Ask:
   - What do you see?
   - What are the caterpillars doing?
   - Do they need their parents to feed them? (As soon as the babies hatched they could start eating because their mother laid the eggs on a leaf she knew they would like to eat. This might lead to a discussion of how children's and adults' tastes in food are different. Often, children like sweets and plain foods, and adults may like spicier foods.)

Chart the Growth and Change of the Caterpillars

Materials

caterpillars in their habitat
poster board
markers

What to Do

1. Make a Growth and Change Chart that begins with today (the day the children first saw the caterpillars) as Day 1, to keep track of when milestones in the life cycle happen.

2. Either the children or teacher can draw a picture of the larvae and record descriptive comments for each day.

3. For each day, also record the number of days that has passed since you began.

4. Use dots to represent the number of days that has passed since observation began. One dot will represent each day. Remember to add dots for the weekend or other skipped days, even though you weren't there to record a picture or an observation. By day 20, you will have 20 dots that can be drawn in groups of five.

What to Talk About

1. Metamorphism means change. Metamorphism for butterflies is the name for the fact that butterflies start out their lives as caterpillars, a very different shape than their parents. Let's check the larvae everyday and record how they change.

2. Ask:
   - How do you think they will change?

Caterpillars Changing into Pupas

Materials

Cabbage White butterfly caterpillars (Pieris rapae) in their habitat or Painted Lady butterfly caterpillars in their container
broccoli or cabbage leaves
water mister

What to Do

1. Continue to maintain the Cabbage White caterpillars and butterflies by supplying them with fresh sugar water and well-washed broccoli leaves or cabbage leaves. Occasionally mist a spot in the habitat so that it does not get too dry. The purchased Painted Lady caterpillars have everything they need in the container they arrived in.

2. Watch for the caterpillars to pupate and form chrysalides (plural of chrysalis). The caterpillar will hang upside down and the skin will change to a protective covering with a few points on it. The Cabbage White chrysalides (pupa) can remain in their habitat. The Painted Lady chrysalides should be moved to a larger container so that when they emerge as butterflies, they can spread their wings. Move the entire paper to which these chrysalides have attached themselves.

What to Talk About

1. Ask:
   - Are the caterpillars changing or getting bigger?
   - What will they look like when they grow up? (The caterpillars have formed chrysalides.)
   - Do you think it is still living inside? What do you think it is doing? (Metamorphism means change. Metamorphism is the name for the fact that butterflies start out as caterpillars and then pupate to become adult butterflies.)

2. Many children and adults are familiar with the term "cocoon," which is the covering moth caterpillars make for themselves when they pupate. If you can find a cocoon, put it in a clear container so the children can compare it to the chrysalides.

3. Ask:
   - What will the insect look like when it comes out, when it emerges from the chrysalis?

Emerging Butterflies

Materials
butterfly chrysalides

What to Do
1. When the butterflies emerge, you may release the Cabbage White butterflies outdoors or continue the cycle. If the Painted Lady butterflies did not come from your neighborhood, they may carry germs that the local Painted Ladies do not have. They should be kept in the indoor habitat for the rest of their lifespan.

What to Talk About
- What do these Cabbage White butterflies need to live? (Now that we have seen their life cycle, from egg to adult, let's release them to the butterfly garden.)
- Whose garden do you think they might visit?
- These Painted Lady butterflies hatched from eggs that were laid in (another state). We will keep them in the habitat as they grow old.
- How long do you think their lifespan is?

Books to Read
Butterfly Gardens, Luring Nature's Loveliest Pollinators to Your Yard edited by Alcinda Lewis

From Caterpillar to Butterfly by Deborah Heiligman, illustrated by Bari Weissman

How to Hide a Butterfly and Other Insects by Ruth Heller

Mealworms, Raise Them, Watch Them, See Them Change by Adrienne Mason, which is not about butterflies but has great illustrations of various animals metamorphosing as they grow to adulthood

Waiting for Wings by Lois Ehlert

Where Butterflies Grow by Joanne Ryder

Follow-Up Activities
- Maintain the butterflies and caterpillars in the classroom.
- Record all the following activities on the calendar: crawling, eating, pooping, growing, hanging upside down, chrysalis formation, butterfly emergence.
- Talk with the children about plants that the caterpillars like to eat and nectar plants for butterflies.
- Eat salad greens, like a caterpillar, and drink sweet juice through straws, like a butterfly.
- Invite the children to make predictions about when chrysalis formation and butterflies emergence will happen, and monitor the caterpillars for these changes.
- Plant a butterfly garden that includes plants for caterpillars to eat and flowering plants for the butterflies. (See "Planting a Butterfly Garden," page 117.)

Bringing Science Home!
A Note Home to Families About the Life Cycle of Butterflies

Dear Families,

The class has started daily observations of caterpillars; at least that is what some of us think they are. The rest of us will decide after we see how the "short fuzzy worms" grow and what they look like when they grow up.

We are watching them move, eat, and grow. Ask your child, "How can you tell they are eating?" We hope to see one complete life cycle of a butterfly, from baby (caterpillar) to teenager (pupa in a chrysalis) to adult (butterfly).

The children have made predictions about how long it will be until they stop growing and are grown up. The older children are recording the growth on a calendar so we can remember how small the caterpillars were when we first saw them—smaller than the smallest pinkie finger! Stop in and observe with us.

Planting a Butterfly Garden

TO GET READY—
Exploring a Butterfly Garden

Order Painted Lady (Vanessa cardui) butterfly caterpillars from a biological supply company or catch Cabbage White (Pieris rapae) butterflies or their caterpillars (see the lesson Butterflies Change as They Grow, pages 108-116). Observe the growth and changes in the larvae, pupa, and adults. Discuss with the children the kinds of food that they like but that their parents do not, and the reverse. Baby butterflies (caterpillars) eat food that is very different from what their parents eat.

What Do Butterflies Eat?

Materials

life cycle chart for butterflies
live butterflies, pupa, or larvae
insect identification book, optional

What to Do

1. Observe some live butterflies, pupa, or larvae, or look at a butterfly life cycle chart. **Note:** See the lesson on butterflies (Butterflies Change as They Grow, pages 108-116) for the names of specific host and nectar plants for the Painted Lady or Cabbage White butterflies. Or read *Butterfly Gardens: Luring Nature's Loveliest Pollinators to Your Yard* edited by Alcinda Lewis, and published by the Brooklyn Botanic Garden.

OBJECTIVES
To recognize that the food needs of larvae and adult butterflies differ
To provide these food sources in the hope of attracting butterflies to the schoolyard

SCIENCE TABLE
Put the following items from the activity on the Science Table. Keep them out for a few weeks, or as long as you are exploring this experience with the children.
♀ Painted Lady (Vanessa cardui) or Cabbage White (Pieris rapae) butterfly larvae in the suggested habitat
♀ Any other caterpillars or butterflies found by the children. If the specific food source for the collected caterpillars or butterflies cannot be identified, the insects should only be kept for two days.

♀ Each science experience has several activities, which, if done in sequence, build on each other.
Doing everything from "To Get Ready" to "Follow-Up Activities" will give children repeated opportunities to understand concepts.
The individual activities can be used separately, and children often want to repeat their favorite activities.

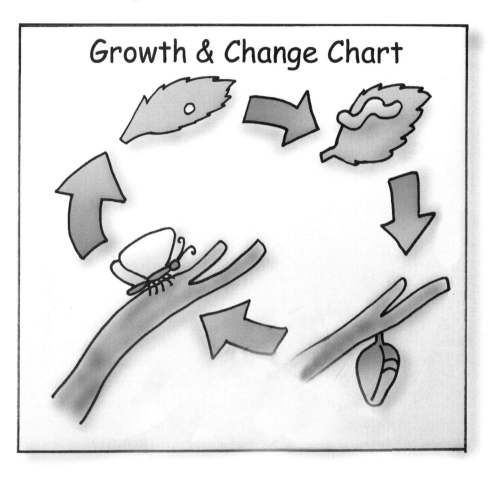

Growth & Change Chart

What to Talk About

1. Ask:
   - ♀ What do you think the caterpillars eat?
   - ♀ What do you think the butterflies eat? (The answers you get might vary widely but accept them all.)
   - ♀ What do their mouths/mouth parts look like?
   - ♀ Which part of the plant do the caterpillars eat?
   - ♀ Which part of the plant do the butterflies eat?
2. Let's observe these animals and watch them to see what they do eat. We could also research the question by looking for the information in an insect identification book.

Taste Butterfly Food

Materials

honeysuckle flowers or sugar and water

What to Do

1. Bring a piece of honeysuckle vine with flowers (if you are confident in your identification), so the children can drink the nectar. This favorite childhood activity involves picking the open flowers, breaking off the end of the tube and sucking on it

to get the tiniest taste of sweetness. The sweetness is the nectar, which is food for butterflies and many other insects, and some birds.

2. If it is not possible to bring in honeysuckle flowers, make a sugar-water solution made by boiling 4 tablespoons water with 1 tablespoon sugar. Keep it refrigerated until you use it.

What to Talk About

1. Ask:
   - ʔ What does butterfly food taste like?
   - ʔ Is it sweet?

Butterfly Tongues

Materials
party favor blowers

What to Do

1. Use a party favor called a blowout (the kind you blow on to unroll a long strip) to be a pretend butterfly tongue. Have one for each child.
2. Encourage the children to make pretend flowers by putting their index fingers and thumbs together to form a circle. Then they can try to fit the "tongue" into the circle to get the nectar. A butterfly tongue is called a *proboscis.*

What to Talk About

1. Say, "Look at my tongue. Will you show me your tongue? How long is it? Is it long enough to reach the nectar inside this flower?"

Plants for Butterflies

Materials
host and nectar plants (or pictures of such plants)
zinnia flower seeds
garden area or container
potting soil, optional

What to Do

1. Examine the plants for your butterfly garden; make sure that some plants are food for the larvae and some are food for the adults of the species of butterfly you are observing in your classroom.
2. Briefly look at all the plants (and/or pictures of them), and have the children divide them into two groups: host plants (for the larvae/caterpillars to eat the leaves) and nectar plants (for the adult butterflies to drink the nectar).
   Note: See the lesson Butterflies Change as They Grow, pages 108-116) for the names of specific host and nectar plants for the Painted Lady or Cabbage White Butterflies. Or read *Butterfly Gardens: Luring Nature's Loveliest Pollinators to Your Yard* edited by Alcinda Lewis, and published by the Brooklyn Botanic Garden.
3. Plant the plants in a sunny spot in the schoolyard, in a barrel planter, window box, or even in a large pot that can be moved, if necessary. Children who do not like to touch dirt can use a stick to plant zinnia seeds.
4. Have the children plant a zinnia seed in a small cup to take home.

What to Talk About

1. The adults and young like to eat different kinds of food. If the children have observed butterflies as they grew from caterpillar to adult butterfly, they might have noticed this. The mouthparts of the adult form (butterfly) are specially shaped to be able to drink the nectar (flower juice) from particular plants. Their babies (larvae) eat the leaves of their favorite plants.

Books to Read

Butterflies in the Garden by Carol Lerner
How to Hide a Butterfly and Other Insects by Ruth Heller
Miss Hallberg's Butterfly Garden by Gay Bishop
The Surprise Garden by Zoe Hall
Waiting for Wings by Lois Ehlert
Where Butterflies Grow by Joanne Ryder

Follow-Up Activity

- Plant a butterfly garden. Label each plant as a host or nectar plant. Unless you are lucky enough to have a large garden, each child cannot plant one or it would be too crowded. Invite the children who don't like to get "yucky" to plant a few zinnia seeds. If you have a large space you could plant a butterfly bush (Buddleia), which flowers during the summer.

If you are raising butterflies, release them (when the nights are warm) near your butterfly garden. Prepare the children to expect the butterflies to fly away to explore. Those butterflies might not visit the butterfly garden again but other butterflies will.

Bringing Science Home!
A Note Home to Families About Planting a Butterfly Garden

Dear Families,

Children are sometimes puzzled when their parents pass up the offer of a sweet treat to eat and parents are sometimes puzzled about how to get their children to eat green vegetables. Butterfly food preferences are the opposite, with adults drinking the sweet flower nectar and the young eating the green leaves.

Providing a food source is part of observing the life cycle of a butterfly. So at school we are planting two kinds of plants for the butterflies: nectar plants for the grownups and host plants for the young, or larvae, to live on and eat. We hope the plants will attract more butterflies to the schoolyard. Have you seen any?

What Is It?

OBJECTIVE
To use our senses of touch and sound, along with logic, to discover the identity of a hidden object

SCIENCE TABLE

Make a matching game. Away from the children, fill three pairs of six opaque containers with the same material, such as cotton balls, pennies, marbles, or bells, and close the lid. Film canisters work well, as do plastic eggs; just make sure to use all the same color eggs to keep the children from using color as a cue or being confused by it. The children shake, turn, and listen to the six small containers and sort them into pairs according to the feel and sound they hear. They can also match them to a card showing what could be inside the container. Make additional pairs with new materials as the children's skills and abilities increase.

TO GET READY—
Exploring the Unknown

Talk about how scientists work to find out about unknown things by looking, weighing, and measuring, and then thinking about what they have learned to make a guess about the nature of the unknown thing.

Seeing and Touching the Choices

Materials
a group of small, familiar objects
a tray

Each science experience has several activities, which, if done in sequence, build on each other. Doing everything from "To Get Ready" to "Follow-Up Activities" will give children repeated opportunities to understand concepts. The individual activities can, of course, be used separately, and children often want to repeat their favorite activities.

What to Do

1. Show the children a tray of three to eight small objects, chosen by you because they are familiar to the children and have a variety of weights and surfaces. Suggestions include a rubber ball, a plastic egg, a square block, a columnar block, a large coin, a small paper cup, a feather, a cotton ball, and a marble.
2. Touch these objects, exploring their properties.

What to Talk About

1. Ask:
   - What do you feel?
   - Is it soft or hard?
   - How heavy is it?
2. Try another object.

What Is It?

Materials

small, familiar objects such as a rubber ball, a plastic egg, a square block, a columnar block, a large coin, a small paper cup, a feather, a cotton ball, and a marble

opaque containers with easily closed lids, such as quart-size plastic yogurt containers or small cardboard boxes

towel

What to Do

1. Tell the children that you'd like to play a game, "What Is It?" with them.
2. Ask them to close their eyes and turn away while you put one of the objects in each container. For groups larger than three, use one container per child, if possible, so they don't have to wait.
3. Spread a towel over the objects so you can secretly slip the objects into the containers, even if the children do peek (which is part of the fun).

Note: Either leave the cloth covering the remaining objects or remove it. Some children will ignore what is left on the table, but others will use viewing what is left on the table as a way of eliminating possibilities, a good strategy. For those children, you might want to keep the remaining objects covered after a few rounds of the game, to make it more challenging.

4. Have each child shake (they will do this naturally) the containers as they listen to the sound the object makes.
5. You may have to encourage them to do a slower form of discovery: turning the container slowly side to side and top to bottom to listen to the object as it moves slowly, and to feel the heft or weight of the contained object. A quarter and a small paper cup sound amazingly alike and weigh about the same amount, but can be distinguished by the way they move.

What to Talk About

1. No peeking! Tell the children that you want them to use other ways than seeing to

decide what is in the container. Don't be too stern about this as peeking is all part of the fun and you can cover the items with a towel to keep them hidden.

2. Ask:
   - What does it sound like?
   - How heavy is it?
   - If it feels heavy, can it be a feather?
   - How does it move?
   - Is it a roller or a slider?

Telling What You Guess

Materials

small, familiar objects
opaque containers with easily closed lids

What to Do

1. Place one object in each container.
2. Play "What Is It?" Give each child a turn to tell his or her guess *before* he or she opens the container.

What to Talk About

1. Say, "Before you open it, tell me what you think is in the container."
2. Ask:
   - Why do you think that?
3. Many children will, for the first round of the game, guess the object that they love best, usually the ball or quarter. Even improbable answers don't need to be corrected. They will soon see if their guess is right. Encourage them to listen to the sound made by each other's containers, to compare to their own.

Repeat the Experience

Materials

small, familiar objects
opaque containers with easily closed lids
a tray
a towel

What to Do

1. Play "What Is It?" again.
2. The children will try different strategies as they repeat the experience.
3. For more of a challenge, put in more than one object and ask the children to guess how many objects are in the container.
4. Play a round where you close your eyes and the children put (usually many) objects into the container for you to guess and identify.

What to Talk About

1. Discuss how it will sound/feel if there are two objects, instead of one, in each container.

Books to Read

ABC Science Riddles by Barbara Saffer
How to Think Like a Scientist: Answering Questions by the Scientific Method by Stephen Kramer
Look Book by Tana Hoban
Mouse Views: What the Classroom Pet Saw by Bruce McMillan
Sense Suspense, a Guessing Game for the Five Senses by Bruce McMillan
When Riddles Come Rumbling: Poems to Ponder by Rebecca Kai Dotlich

Follow-Up Activities

- Encourage the children to do the activity at home with their families.
- Let each child make a "What Is It?" game to take home using small yogurt containers or small milk cartons. A small bag could hold the container, a cotton ball and a ping-pong ball or plastic egg, for example. Write "What Is It?" on the bag and have the children explain it to their families.

Bringing Science Home!
A Note Home to Families About "What Is It?"

Dear Families,

I once watched a group of children from a television science program challenge a Nobel Prize winner, chemist Linus Pauling, to discover what object they had put in a small box without opening it! As he shook and turned the box he listened to the sounds and told the children what he was thinking. His passion for discovering the unknown was obvious. Today your children expressed the same enthusiasm while they did a similar exercise. Ask your child to play "What Is It?" with you by putting a small object into a container and having you figure out what it could be. Feel the weight, shake it, and turn it, but don't peek! What is it?

Rocks Made of Tiny Pieces
(Sedimentary Rocks)

OBJECTIVE
To notice the range in grain size in sedimentary rocks (rocks made of tiny pieces)

SCIENCE TABLE
Put a tray of sedimentary rocks on the Science Table. Smaller rocks can be glued to a board to keep them out of children's mouths. Keep them out for a few weeks, or as long as you are exploring this experience with the children.

TO GET READY—

Exploring Sedimentary Rocks

Materials
rocks

What to Do
1. Ask the children if they would like to start a rock collection.
2. Ask each child to bring in a found (but not precious) rock.
3. Encourage the children to compare the rocks to each other in color, size, weight, and texture. Note that a rock can be many sizes and have different names and still be a rock, such as sand, pebble, stone, and boulder.

Each science experience has several activities, which, if done in sequence, build on each other.
Doing everything from "To Get Ready" to "Follow-Up Activities" will give children repeated opportunities to understand concepts.
The individual activities can be used separately, and children often want to repeat their favorite activities.

Comparing Rocks

Materials

variety of sedimentary rocks
rock identification book (see Books to Read, page 129)

What to Do

1. Acquire a variety of sedimentary rocks (such as conglomerate, sandstone, and shale) for the children to look at and handle. A sedimentary rock is one that is made of little pieces that were moved from one place to another before being cemented together. Sandstone is made of tiny grains that were eroded from another rock and moved to a new place, such as a beach or streambed.
2. Compare the actual rocks to those pictured in the identification books.
   Note: Depending on your local geology, you can find sedimentary rocks in the streambeds or in tilled fields. Some graveled driveways may contain sandstone and shale pebbles, or look in

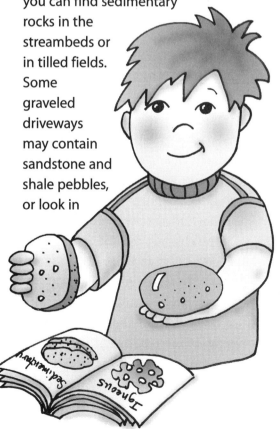

the telephone book for stone dealers. Small collections of rocks can be ordered from scientific supply companies. An identification book such as the *Golden Guide* or the *Eyewitness Handbook,* both titled *Rocks and Minerals,* can help you identify rocks.

What to Talk About

1. Ask:
   - How do these rocks feel?
   - What size are the pieces that make up these rocks?
   - Can you see them or feel them?
   - Are any of these rocks the same?
   - How are they different?
   - Can you find this one in the book?

Feel the Ingredients of Rocks

Materials

sand
clay
spoons
bowls or newspaper
paper towels

What to Do

1. Dampen the sand to make it easy to scoop.
2. If the clay is not soft enough to scoop, put it in a bowl or plastic bag with some water and let it sit for a day or until it can be spooned up.
3. Present the materials in separate bowls or spread newspapers over a table so the children can mix, knead, and sculpt while they feel it.
4. Encourage the children to feel the clay and experience its smoothness.
5. Then encourage them to feel the sand.

3. Have small samples of clay and sand for the children to refer to.
   Note: Some graveled driveways may contain sandstone and shale pebbles, or look in the telephone book for stone dealers.

What to Talk About

1. Ask:
   - Which one was made from clay and which one was made from sand? (The sandstone was made from sand and the shale was made from clay.)

Mixing Up a Pretend Rock

Materials

damp sand
wet clay
pebbles, shells, or dirt, optional
small paper cups
craft sticks
plaster of Paris
disposable containers in which to mix plaster
water

What to Do

1. Label each cup with a child's name.
2. Give each child a paper cup (with his or her name on it), and ask the children to fill their cup about 1/2 full of damp sand or very wet clay. They can also add pebbles, shells, or dirt.
3. Help the children mix these materials and then add a heaping tablespoon of mixed plaster of Paris (see instructions on page 129).
4. Stir the mixture with a craft stick until well mixed. (Since most children like to have a mixture of some of everything, make one pretend rock of just clay and one of just sand so the children can compare these "rocks" after they dry.)

6. Encourage reluctant children to touch with just one finger and provide paper towels for wiping off the clay.

What to Talk About

1. Ask:
   - What do you think this is? (Some rocks are made of these little pieces.)
   - How are they alike?
   - How are they different?
   - Where have you seen clay or sand?
   - How does it get there?
   - What size are the pieces that make up the clay and sand?

Feel the Difference Between Two Kinds of Rocks

Materials

samples of sandstone, shale, clay, and sand

What to Do

1. Look at and feel sandstone.
2. Look at and feel shale.

What to Talk About

1. Ask:
   - Would you like to make a pretend sedimentary rock?
   - What does your mixture look like?
   - Is it easy or hard to mix it all together? (Younger children will need help mixing it completely.)
   - Is it hard yet? (A special cement, called plaster of Paris, glues all the little clay and sand pieces together as it dries.)

2. Rock making is happening all the time, not in schools or factories but in nature—outside on our Earth. It takes a long time for the sand grains to get all piled up in the same place; and another long time for water, carrying dissolved minerals that will be the glue that holds the sand grains together, to wash down into the sand and harden. It will take a shorter time for our pretend rock to be cemented into stone. Our pretend rocks will be done by tomorrow or the next time we come to school.

Books to Read

The Pebble in My Pocket: A History of Our Earth by Meredith Hooper

Peterson First Guide to Rocks and Minerals by Frederick H. Pough

Planet Earth/Inside Out by Gail Gibbons

Rocks and Minerals by Joel Arem

Simon and Schuster's Guide to Rocks and Minerals by Martin Prinz, George Harlow and Joseph Peters

Solid, Liquid, or Gas? by Fay Robinson

Follow-Up Activities

- Peel off the paper cup to reveal the pretend sedimentary rock. Doing this as a group will get the children comparing rocks and talking about how these rocks are made of different-size pieces.
- Make an edible sedimentary rock using a Rice Krispies® treats recipe but substituting a variety of cereals.

MIXING PLASTER OF PARIS

Note: *Keep the plaster out of reach of children. All mixing should be done by an adult away from the children. Read the instructions on the package before starting. The plaster powder is very fine and lifts into the air very easily. It is not good to breathe in any kind of dust.*

Materials

plaster of Paris
disposable container, such as a milk jug or juice carton
scoop
water
rubber glove or large spoon

What to Do

1. For a group of 12 children, mix up about two cups of plaster.
2. Use a disposable container such as a plastic milk jug or juice carton, opened at the top, for mixing the plaster.
3. Carefully scoop the plaster powder into the container, leaving room to add water.
4. Start with less water than you think you will need, using your hand (covered with a rubber glove) or a large spoon to mix and smash big lumps.
5. Add more water, a little at a time, until a smooth paste is formed.
6. When it is ready to be added to the children's rock mixtures, the plaster will be the consistency of pancake batter or a milkshake.
7. Even though the plaster will harden within 30 minutes, let the pretend rocks sit for 24 hours before peeling off the paper cups. Otherwise, some of the clay may still be wet.
8. Tools and hands can be washed off with water.
   Note: Do not pour any remaining plaster down the sink. Throw it into the trash.

Bringing Science Home!
A Note Home to Families About Rocks Made of Tiny Pieces (Sedimentary Rocks)

Dear Families,
Picking up a rock is almost irresistible. Once it's in your hand you might notice its texture, color, and weight. Children love classifying them, putting all of the flat ones in a group and the pink ones in another. One day the smooth ones are the favorites and the next day the round ones are the best. Maybe you can see tiny little pieces in it, like grains of sand. How was this rock made anyway? If the rock is made of sand it is a sedimentary rock, one that is made of little pieces that were moved from one place to another before being cemented together.

The children handled several pieces of sedimentary rock and the raw ingredients for some of them—sand (tiny pieces) and clay (even tinier pieces). Then we made pretend rocks out of sand, clay, and/or pebbles mixed with plaster of Paris. It took only a few hours for these pretend rocks to become hard.

We talked about how rock making is happening all the time, not in schools or factories but in nature, outside on our Earth. It takes a long time for the sand grains to get all piled up in the same place. And another long time for water, carrying dissolved minerals that will be the glue, to wash down into the sand and harden.

Would you like to bring in a rock of any kind for the class' collection?

Rocks That Were Melted (Igneous Rocks) and Volcanoes

TO GET READY—
Exploring Igneous Rocks

Materials
papier-mâché recipe on page 211
plastic juice bottle
scissors
hot glue gun (adult only)
small container, such as a film canister
tempera or acrylic paint
paintbrush
polyurethane (adult only)
Hill of Fire by Thomas Lewis
non-fiction books about volcanoes

What to Do
1. Making a model of a volcano is optional, but worth the time spent. Small cups may be used in place of the model. One month before, make a model of a volcano using the papier-mâché recipe in the Recycling Paper lesson (pages 207-213). (It takes a week or more for the thick papier-mâché to dry, and a day to dry between each paint/waterproofing coating.) This model will last for years and will withstand many eruptions so it's worth the initial effort.

2. As a base for the papier-mâché, use the cone-shaped top half of a plastic juice bottle. Use a hot glue gun to glue a small container, such as a film canister, into the mouth of the juice bottle to hold the baking soda.

OBJECTIVES
To learn about volcanoes
To combine two substances and observe a chemical change

SCIENCE TABLE
Put a variety of volcanic rocks on your Science Table. Keep them out for a few weeks, or as long as you are exploring this experience with the children.

Each science experience has several activities, which, if done in sequence, build on each other.
Doing everything from "To Get Ready" to "Follow-Up Activities" will give children repeated opportunities to understand concepts.
The individual activities can, of course, be used separately, and children often want to repeat their favorite activities.

3. Cover the sides of the bottle with about a half inch of papier-mâché paste. Smaller models can be made by surrounding just a film canister with the papier-mâché in the shape of a cone.

4. Before painting, let it dry thoroughly. Paint the volcano with tempera or acrylic paints and again, let it dry thoroughly.

5. Waterproof the volcano with several coats of polyurethane covering (adult only), available from craft or paint stores.

6. A day before doing the erupting experience, read the book *Hill of Fire* by Thomas Lewis, an easy reader set in Mexico, to the children.

7. Introduce the idea of volcanoes by using books with photographs from the non-fiction section of the library. Just have the books available to the children in the book area—it's not necessary to read them.

Touch Volcanic Rocks

Materials
volcanic rocks

What to Do
1. Encourage the children to look at and handle volcanic rocks, such as hardened and cooled lava or pumice. If none of the children comment, point out the holes in the rock.
   Note: A volcanic rock called pumice can be purchased in the nail care aisle of a drugstore or from scientific supply companies.

What to Talk About
1. Ask:
   - How did these holes get in the rock? (Gas, like air, made these bubbles and

the rock got cool and hard before the bubbles popped, leaving holes.)
   - How can we tell if these rocks were melted? (Sometimes you can see an obvious drip marking in the rock.)

LAVA ROCKS

Experiencing Baking Soda and Vinegar Separately

Materials
baking soda
vinegar
two small bowls
small scoop
small pitcher
two craft sticks or spoons for each child
towels
bucket for waste liquid if there is no sink nearby

What to Do

1. Look at baking soda and vinegar (set out in two dishes).
2. Use craft sticks to take tiny tastes of the baking soda and the vinegar. For younger children, serve the tastes.
3. Invite the children to feel the dry baking soda and wet vinegar.

What to Talk About

1. Talk about never tasting something unless you know what it is, or an adult who you trust says it's safe. Assure them that you would never give them something to taste that could hurt them.
2. Ask:
   - Do they taste the same or different?
   - Are they wet or dry?
   - Are they moving?
   - What do you think will happen when we mix them together?
   - Why?

Going to the Pretend Volcano

Materials
hard hats and mittens, optional
volcano form or small cup

What to Do

1. If you have them, put on hard hats and mittens and pretend they are the protective clothing needed to get ready to go close to a volcano.
2. Look at the pretend volcano. Use a model of a volcano that you made ahead or use a small paper cup. Use the words "cone" (the mountain) and "crater" (hole where the lava comes out).

What to Talk About

1. Ask:
   - Have you ever seen a volcano?
   - Where in the world are volcanoes? (Some places are the northwest coast of the United States, Hawaii, Iceland, and Central America.)
   - Why would we need protection for our body if we wanted to get close to a real volcano? (Real volcanoes are very hot.) This is a pretend volcano, a model of a real one, and will not be hot.

Erupting the Volcano

Materials
volcano form or small cup
large bowl to hold the "volcano"
baking soda
vinegar
small scoop
small pitcher
towels
bucket for waste liquid if there is not a sink nearby

What to Do

1. Erupt a pretend volcano.
2. Have the children scoop the baking soda into the "vent."
3. Ask:
   - What do you think will happen if we mix this liquid vinegar into the dry baking soda?
4. Have the children take turns pouring the vinegar into the vent. Many children will pour until the pitcher is empty so fill it with a small amount for each child.
5. Notice the bubbles.
6. Notice the flow.
7. Be prepared to continue this activity for some time because the children love it.

What to Talk About

1. Ask:
   - ⚲ What do you think will happen?
   - ⚲ What do you see?

   The volcanic rock we looked at has holes in it. We saw bubbles in the pretend lava that flowed out of our volcano.

Books to Read

Hill of Fire by Thomas Lewis
Planet Earth/Inside Out by Gail Gibbons
Solid, Liquid, or Gas? by Fay Robinson

Follow-Up Activity

⚲ Once is not enough with the "erupting" part of this experiment. On a nice day, it can be done outside with the whole class.

Bringing Science Home!
A Note Home to Families About Rocks That Were Melted (Igneous Rocks) and Volcanoes

Dear Families,

The objectives of this lesson are to learn about volcanoes and to combine two substances and observe a chemical change. These objectives do not convey the thrill the children experienced when they erupted our pretend volcano. Their imaginations were in high gear and their senses engaged.

We got ready by looking at pictures of volcanoes, handling volcanic rocks, and tasting the baking soda and vinegar before we mixed the two substances together to cause an eruption of "lava."

Volcanoes can be a serious natural disaster, far from child's play. The book, Hill of Fire *by Thomas Lewis, tells how one child's community handled the danger and disruption of a volcano's birth in their fields.*

The volcanic rocks we handled were not hot. Could it be that they were once hot enough to melt?

Fossil Discovery

TO GET READY—
Exploring Fossils

Materials
books about fossils, such as:
> *Fossils Tell of Long Ago* by Aliki
> *It Could Still Be a Rock* by Alan Fowler

molds

playdough or polymer clay

What to Do

1. Talk with the children about the fact that there were other ancient life forms besides dinosaurs that sometimes became fossilized.

2. Read (parts of) *Fossils Tell of Long Ago* by Aliki, *It Could Still Be a Rock* by Alan Fowler, or another fossil book.

3. Look in the non-fiction section of the public library for books that are picture galleries of fossils.

4. Use molds and playdough or polymer clay purchased at a craft store to make casts (shapes made by filling in the molds).

OBJECTIVES
To introduce the idea of fossils being a record of early life.
To experience making imprints and casts (shapes made by filling in the imprints with plaster)

SCIENCE TABLE
Put the items listed below on the Science Table. Keep them out for a few weeks, or as long as you are exploring this experience with the children.

- *the children's plaster impressions (made during this lesson)*
- *any fossil that isn't precious*
- *playdough*

 Each science experience has several activities, which, if done in sequence, build on each other.
Doing everything from "To Get Ready" to "Follow-Up Activities" will give children repeated opportunities to understand concepts.
The individual activities can, of course, be used separately, and children often want to repeat their favorite activities.

Matching Objects to Their Imprints in Playdough

Materials

homemade playdough (see recipe below)

large disposable tray

plaster of Paris

container for mixing plaster

plaster casts of dog footprints

various fossils

some living things, such as a leaf or flower

PLAYDOUGH RECIPE

Materials

2 cups water

2 cups flour

1 cup salt

4 teaspoons cream of tartar

2 tablespoons vegetable oil

mixing cups and spoons

saucepan

stove or hot plate (adult only)

food coloring, optional

What to Do

1. To make playdough, mix ingredients together in a saucepan.
2. Cook over low heat, stirring constantly, until the mixture forms a ball.
3. Remove from heat, cool, and knead.
4. Add food coloring, if desired.

What to Do

1. When the children are not around, press a foot (dog or human), a shell, a dried ear of corn, a pinecone, or any other interesting and somewhat familiar natural object into homemade playdough (see recipe).

2. Encourage the children to look at these imprints carefully and try to guess what living thing made each imprint (shape pressed into the dough).

3. Then reveal the actual objects, and have the children try to match the objects with their imprints.

PLASTER CASTS OF FOOTPRINTS

To make a plaster cast of an animal foot, have the pet step into a tray of playdough. Mix a small amount of plaster of Paris (see Mixing Plaster of Paris, page129) and pour it into the footprint in the playdough. When it has dried completely, remove from the dough. Then oil the surface with mineral oil to keep it from sticking in playdough when you use it to make imprints.

What to Talk About

1. Ask:
   - Who made this imprint? (Some fossils are imprints. Fossils are clues to help us learn what happened on the Earth before people were here.)
   - Who lived on the Earth before we lived here?

Make Imprints in Playdough

Materials

homemade playdough (recipe on page 137)
large disposable tray
living things, such as a leaf or flower
objects from the classroom

What to Do

1. Gather around a huge tray of playdough.
2. Encourage the children to each make an imprint in the dough using their hands, if they are willing.

3. The children may want to use classroom objects, such as blocks or toy animals.
4. Make additional imprints of other living things, such as a leaf, a flower, or an animal footprint (see directions on page 137).

What to Talk About

1. The impressions are shapes of whatever was pressed into the dough. The dough is soft.
2. Ask:
   - Did you ever make a footprint in the mud or sand? (Imprints can also be made in mud and sand.)

Preserving the Imprints With Plaster

Materials

imprints from previous activity
plaster of Paris (see recipe on page 129)
small plastic toy animal

What to Do

1. Without the children, mix a batch of plaster of Paris (see instructions on page 129).
2. Tell and/or act out the story in the following "What to Talk About" section.
3. While the children are watching, pour the plaster on top of the imprints in playdough. Allow 24 hours for the plaster to harden before removing the playdough to reveal the shapes of the imprints.

What to Talk About

1. Before pouring the plaster, tell a story about how fossils are sometimes formed as you act it out using toy animals.

Once upon a time, a long time ago, a turtle (or other animal) walked through the mud at the edge of a river. Sometimes footprints in the sand or mud get covered up by more sand or more mud. Suddenly a flood of water came down the river pushing lots of sand with it. The footprints made in the mud got covered up and, over a long time, became a rock. Because they turned into a rock, they lasted a long time and we can still see them. These are called fossils. Fossils are remains of plants or animals that lived a long time ago that have turned to rock.

2. When it is ready to be poured over the playdough, the plaster will be the consistency of pancake batter or a milkshake.
3. Pour it over the playdough, filling all the imprints.
4. Even though the plaster will harden within 30 minutes, let it sit for 24 hours before peeling the playdough from the hardened plaster. Otherwise, the playdough will stick to the plaster.
5. Wash tools and hands with water.
   Note: Do not pour any remaining plaster down the sink. Throw it into the trash.

Handling Real Fossils

Materials
various fossils

What to Do
1. Provide a variety of fossils to look at and handle. (They can be purchased at gem and mineral shows or stores, or through scientific supply catalogues.)
2. Ask the children to identify them or speculate on what the fossil was like when it was alive.

What to Talk About
1. Ask:
   - What do you think this fossil was when it was a living thing?
   - Was it an animal or plant?
   - Does it look familiar? Where do you think it lived (in the ocean, near a river, in a forest or grassland)?

   Now the plant or animal shape has become rock.

Books to Read
Footprints in the Snow by Cynthia Benjamin
Fossils Tell of Long Ago by Aliki
Look in the non-fiction section of the public library for books of photographs or illustrations of fossils.

Follow-Up Activities
- Make individual hand, foot, elbow, or other body part imprints in playdough or sand.
- Fill them with plaster to make the imprint shapes permanent.

Bringing Science Home!
A Note Home to Families About Fossil Discovery

Dear Families,
Fossils are the remains of plants or animals that lived a long time ago that have turned into rock. They are clues to help us learn what happened on the Earth before people were here.

To make our pretend fossils, we first made marks, or imprints, in a pan of playdough. Some of us used our fingers, others "walked" toy animals (yes, there were some dinosaurs) through the dough, and still others used interesting objects from the classroom to make imprints.

We told a story about how a scene like this might have happened a long time ago when a real fossil was made:

Once upon a time, a long time ago, an animal walked through the mud at the edge of a river. Sometimes footprints in mud, or sand, get covered up by more sand or mud. Suddenly a flood of water came down the river pushing lots of mud with it. The footprints made in the mud were covered up and then got hard and turned into rock. Because they turned into rock they lasted a long time and we can still see them. They are called fossils.

We filled our imprints with wet plaster of Paris. Then we took the playdough off the plaster to see our pretend fossils!

Mirrors Reflect

TO GET READY—

Exploring Mirrors

Materials

flashlights
unbreakable mirrors (Plexiglas mirrors, about 3" x 5" and without a frame, are ideal)
a dark place (see suggestions below)
index cards
markers

What to Do

1. Use the word "reflect" when observing children in the housekeeping area in front of the mirror, when passing by a storefront window, or looking in a puddle.
2. As an introduction to the movement of light, set up a flashlight center in a dark area with flashlights and mirrors. The dark area could be simply a sheet of black construction paper, the space underneath a table that is covered with a tablecloth, or a box large enough to fit both a child's head and flashlight. This setup will provide the materials needed for the children to discover that light travels in a straight line and is reflected by a mirror.
3. Teach the children that they should never shine a flashlight in their own faces or anyone else's face.
4. Play a "making whole" mirror game. Make a set of cards showing partial images (or half of a pair of something) that can be "made whole" using small Plexiglas mirrors held perpendicularly to the card. The images can

OBJECTIVES

To experiment with light

To notice that light travels in a straight line and reflects from surfaces

SCIENCE TABLE

Put the periscopes, both purchased and made (see page 145), on the Science Table. Keep them out for a few weeks, or as long as you are exploring this experience with the children.

Each science experience has several activities, which, if done in sequence, build on each other. Doing everything from To Get Ready to Follow-Up Activities will give children repeated opportunities to understand concepts. The individual activities can, of course, be used separately, and children often want to repeat their favorite activities.

be half a butterfly, half a face, a single shoe, a broken dish, one eye, a partially deflated balloon, and so on. By holding the mirror upright so one edge lies on the card and perpendicular to it, the image reflected in the mirror completes the picture, making the object whole or the pair complete. Introduce it to the children by saying, "Oh no, I lost one of my shoes! Can you help me find the other one by using the mirror?"

What Do We See in a Mirror?

Materials

Plexiglas mirrors

What to Do

1. Look into mirrors. Try to have one mirror (Plexiglas) per child.
   Note: Plexiglas mirrors are relatively expensive but as a unique and durable material, they are worth the expense. To save money, large pieces of Plexiglas mirrors can be special ordered from a plastics company and cut at school by a handy person who has experience cutting glass. The sharp edges of the freshly cut glass can be filed down by careful rubbing on cement sidewalks or with a file. Larger pieces are wonderful surfaces to use for making fingerpainting prints.

What to Talk About

1. Say, "I see…me! Do you see me?"
2. Ask:
   - What else do you see in the mirror?
   - Is that object/person in front of you, next to you, or behind you?

Predicting Where Light Will Travel

Materials

bright flashlight
sheet of black paper

What to Do

1. Shine a flashlight so that it "tickles" each child on the hands or knees. Turn off the overhead lights if you can't see the beam clearly. The light beam will be easier to see if you shine the flashlight onto a sheet of black paper.
2. Turn on the flashlight and point it down at the table. Ask the children to make a prediction before turning it on. (See the suggested questions in "What to Talk About," below.)
3. Turn off the flashlight and point it up to the ceiling. Ask the children to make a prediction before turning it on. (See the suggested questions in "What to Talk About," below.)
4. This teacher-directed introduction to the movement of light is intended to be a review of the children's earlier discovery, using a flashlight, that light travels in a straight line.

What to Talk About

1. Ask:
   - Which way is the flashlight pointing?
   - Where will the light beam go or shine?
   - Is that where you thought it would go?

Exploring How a Mirror Affects the Direction of Light

Materials

bright flashlight
Plexiglas mirror

What to Do

1. Hold up a Plexiglas mirror facing down to the table and point the flashlight up at it. Ask the suggested questions before turning the flashlight on.

What to Talk About

1. Ask:
   - Is the flashlight pointing up or down?
   - Where do you think the light beam will go?
   - Is that where you thought the light would go?

Where Does the Light Go?

Materials

sheet of black paper
bright flashlight, one for each child if possible
Plexiglas mirrors

What to Do

1. Turn a flashlight on and use a mirror to bounce light from the flashlight to each child, to the black paper, and then all around the room.

2. With older children you can move the light spot more quickly and they will still be able to follow it with their eyes.

3. After doing this activity with one flashlight, if possible, provide a flashlight for each child to use. Remind them that the rule is "Never shine a flashlight in your own or anyone else's face."

What to Talk About

1. Ask:
   - Is that where you thought the light was going to shine?
   - How did it get there? (The light is going to the mirror, bouncing off the mirror, and then going to the floor, black paper, knees, and so on.)

2. Trace the path of the light beam with your finger if the children are unable to do so. Light bounces off surfaces. It reflects strongly from surfaces that are smooth and do not break up the light wave and scatter it.

Light Reflects Off Surfaces and Onto Others

Materials

very brightly colored (fluorescent) foamboard or stiff paper

small pieces (4" x 4") of the same brightly colored paper

What to Do

1. Hold up a piece of very brightly colored paper (such as fluorescent pink) and try to wipe the color off onto your clothes and skin.

2. Now hold the paper at an angle under your chin so that the children can see the color reflected onto your skin and lips.

3. Give each child a small piece of the same very brightly colored paper to hold under his or her chin. While looking at their neighbor or in a small mirror, they can see if the color reflects onto their lips and chins. When I was a child we used to hold a bright yellow flower, such as a buttercup or dandelion, under our chins and check to see if we "liked butter" (the yellow color was reflected onto our skin).

What to Talk About

1. Ask:
   - Does the color come off onto my shirt or my hand?
   - What color can you see on our chins?

- How did it get there? (Light reflects off surfaces.)

Use a Mirror to See Around Corners

Materials

large piece of cardboard
Plexiglas mirrors

What to Do

1. Hold up a large "wall" of cardboard and hide behind it.

2. Then hold up a mirror at one edge of the wall so that half the mirror is behind the wall and half is in front of the wall. By looking in the mirror from your position behind the wall, you can see anything that is in front of the wall. Look at each child in turn.

What to Talk About

1. Ask:
   - Can we see around corners?
   - What can we sense around corners without going around the corners ourselves? I can touch you (feel with your hand), and I can hear you (put one ear around the edge of the wall), and if you're wearing perfume I can smell you (sniff loudly). I can see you when I use a mirror!

Use a Periscope

Materials

periscopes, purchased or made (see next page)

What to Do

1. A periscope is a tool that uses two mirrors to see around corners.

2. Give the children periscopes to discover how to use them to see around a corner.

What to Talk About

1. Ask:
   - ℘ What do you see?
   - ℘ How many mirrors are needed?

Make a Periscope

Materials

2 cardboard milk cartons
2 small, rectangular mirrors
scissors or box cutter
tape
Plexiglas mirrors, small enough to fit inside the milk cartons

What to Do

1. Make periscopes using two cardboard half-gallon or quart-size milk cartons, two small rectangular mirrors, and packing tape.
2. Open the tops of the cartons completely.
3. Cut a square hole on one side of each carton, about ½" from the bottom. The hole should go all the way across one side of the carton and an equal height up, to form a square.
4. Position the cartons together so the open tops are touching and the cut holes are on opposite sides.
5. Overlap the tops and tape them together. The body of the periscope, formed by the two cartons, needs to be fairly straight to give a clear view.
6. Now put each mirror in through a cut hole and tape the front edge of the mirror just inside the carton, at the opening of each hole.
7. Tape the opposite edge of the mirror against the far wall of the carton so the mirror rests at an angle.

8. When both mirrors are in place you should be able to look into one and see what is reflected in the other. You may have to fiddle with the angle of the mirrors or straighten the cartons to get the best view.

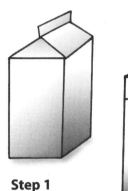

Step 1

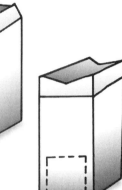

Step 2

Step 3

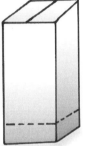

Step 4

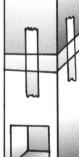

Step 6

Step 5

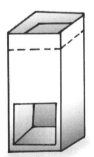

Step 7

Use a Flexible Mirror

Materials
mirrored acetate
Plexiglas mirror

What to Do
1. Give the children small squares of mirrored acetate (sold as wrapping paper) and ask them to find their faces in it as they bend it. For children who put things in their mouths, use one large sheet.

What to Talk About
1. Ask:
   - How are these two mirrors different (Plexiglas and acetate)?
   - Why do we look funny in the acetate mirror? (Our image is distorted in the acetate mirror because it bends.) Demonstrate the bending; it is more important that they see it happen than hear the explanation.

Books to Read
I See Me by Pegi Deitz Shea
Reflections by Ann Jonas
Shadows and Reflections by Tana Hoban

Follow-Up Activities
- Use the periscopes to see around corners, from underneath tables, and behind your back.
- Use periscopes on the playground to play "I Spy" games.
- Make mirror image paintings by painting on a paper with a fold down the center, fold it in half while it's still wet, press lightly all over, and open to dry. This is a great way to make butterflies!
- Fill a dark-colored bowl with water and look for reflections, inside or outside the school.

Bringing Science Home!
A Note Home to Families About Mirrors

Dear Families,

As we explored and discovered the properties of mirrors, the children moved their mirrors around to flash light across the room, to peek at their faces, and to make room for their friend's face in the mirror. When they can control the materials in their environment, they learn so much.

Mirrors weren't the only surface we used to reflect or bounce light to another place. Bright pink cardboard, held under our chins, bounced pink light up to cover our chins and lips with a soft pink glow. Did you ever do that when you were a child with yellow buttercups or dandelions?

Working With Pumps, Siphons, and Capillary Action

(This is best done outside, at the water table, or with plenty of towels.)

OBJECTIVES

To explore moving water—what's gravity got to do with it?

To raise the question of what forces move water in a variety of situations

SCIENCE TABLE

Put the following items on the Science Table. Keep them out for a few weeks, or as long as you are exploring this experience with the children.

- *An egg timer/hour glass with sand or colored liquid inside to observe gravity at work*
- *Two hard-to-spill dishes, such as plastic water bowls for pets or short square tubs, and small tools for moving water, such as spoons, eyedroppers, and scoops*

Each science experience has several activities, which, if done in sequence, build on each other.
Doing everything from "To Get Ready" to "Follow-Up Activities" will give children repeated opportunities to understand concepts.
The individual activities can, of course, be used separately, and children often want to repeat their favorite activities.

TO GET READY—

Exploring Pumps, Siphons, and Capillary Action

Materials

pump, such as a liquid soap pump

What to Do

1. Before introducing the activities in this science experience, comment, perhaps during snack, about how the beverage always goes down from the pitcher—not up, not sideways, but down every time.

2. Introduce the word *gravity*, a force that works to pull things to the earth.

3. Use a pump, such as a liquid soap pump, to help older children discover that the liquid inside must go up (from the bottom of the container through the tube to the opening) to come out. This position is opposite of how they hold a bottle when they pour a liquid out.

4. An inexpensive way to allow the children to repeatedly use the liquid soap container is to fill it with colored water.

Move the Water

Materials

2 short tubs, preferably square or rectangular
water
food coloring
4 clear toy pumps
eyedroppers, also known as medicine droppers
spoons or scoops
towels

What to Do

1. Give the children the task of moving the water from one container to another. Square plastic tubs work well because they can be placed side by side with little gap for spillage and they don't tip easily.

2. Provide some spoons or scoops to work with first, then make eyedroppers available (the children may need instruction to use them), and finally, introduce the children to the clear pumps.
   Note: The plastic toy pumps can be found at toy stores or in the science section of school supply stores and/or catalogues.

3. Coloring the water makes it easier to see. Have plenty of towels on hand.

What to Talk About

1. Ask:
   - What tool works to transfer the water?
   - What tool is easiest to use?
   - What tool is quickest?
   - Who or what is doing the work to move the water? (We use our muscles to lift up the water with the spoons, and gravity does the work to make it fall into the second container.)

2. We use the word *gravity* to name the force that works to pull things to the earth. What else does gravity pull to the earth?

How Do Pumps Work?

Materials
4 clear, toy pumps

What to Do
1. Look at the pump closely.

What to Talk About
1. Ask:
   - ☝ Do the parts of the pump move up or down?
   - ☝ How do you think this moves the water?
   - ☝ Does pushing or pulling have anything to do with it?
   - ☝ Does the pump move the water by itself or does gravity help it?

   The children may not have answers to these questions. That's okay, it's enough to just get them started wondering.

Siphons Work With Suction and Gravity

Materials
2 clear, empty juice bottles
2-foot length of clear tubing
water
food coloring
towels
bleach solution (¼ cup bleach in a gallon of water)

What to Do
1. This amazing way of using first suction and then gravity's work of pulling, fascinates children as they try to figure out how siphoning works. Have the children help by holding the bottles or the ends of the tubes to keep the water from spilling.
2. Demonstrate siphoning by using two clear juice bottles, (quart or gallon size so they won't tip over easily) and a length of clear plastic tubing (like a straw but flexible), about two feet long.
   Note: The tubing can be purchased at hardware stores.
3. Fill one bottle halfway with colored water, put one end of the tube down into the water, and elevate that bottle.
4. Suck on the other end of the tube until water reaches your lips and then quickly put your thumb over the end and put it down into the empty bottle.
5. To make the water flow from the full bottle to the empty one, the end of the tube in the empty bottle must be lower than the end in the water.
6. Watch the water flow from the elevated bottle through the tube into the lower bottle. If it does not, it's probably because air got into the tube before the outgoing end was lower than the intake end. Try again and be sure that no bubbles get in the tube from the end in your mouth before you put it in the lower container. Practice!
7. Then have older children try it with their own tubes. Very few will be able to get a flow going but they will have fun trying.
8. Clean all tubes with bleach solution and rinse well before the next use.

What to Talk About
1. Ask:
   - ☝ Does the water move up or down?
   - ☝ What makes the water move?
   - ☝ Does something push it? Pull it?
   - ☝ Who (or what) is doing the work to move the water?

Capillary Action in Paper

Materials

water
clear plastic containers
coffee filters
food coloring

What to Do

1. Color water with food coloring, creating a dark color.
2. Give each child a strip cut from a coffee filter.
3. Have them dip just an edge into a container of darkly colored water and then take the coffee filter out of the water.
4. Ask them to hold the filters with the wet edge down.
5. Tell them to watch closely, and that the process will take a few minutes.

What to Talk About

1. Ask:
   - Do you think you can make water flow up?
   - What do you see happening? (The water will go up in the paper.)
   - Does the water move? In what directions?
   - Who (or what) is doing the work to move the water? (The tiny pieces of water that can get into the tiny spaces in the paper are small enough to be drawn upwards by being attracted to the sides of the paper fibers.)

An alternative to the plastic toy pumps is to make the pump described in *How Things Work* by Neil Ardley. The advantage of this pump is that less water gets spilled when using it. Children love the feel of the balloon as they push it down, and the sound the balloon makes as it comes up—like breathing! It is easy and inexpensive to make, but acquiring the needed materials takes some time. Punching ball balloons are more durable than the suggested regular balloons. Ball bearings can be purchased at a bike repair shop and the clear tubing from a hardware store. The best plastic containers are the ones restaurants use for carryout soups. Hot glue from a glue gun holds it all together, especially if you also glue the containers to a board.

Capillary Action in Plants

Materials

water
clear plastic containers
white carnations
food coloring

What to Do

1. Early in the week, set up this carnation in colored water experiment.
2. Put quite a lot of food coloring into water in a clear jar.
3. Cut off several inches from the bottom of the stem of a white carnation and then put it into the jar.
4. Observe it every day to see if the food coloring can be seen in the petals.
5. If you want to get fancy, use two jars and two colors, and split the carnation stem between the two jars of colored water.

What to Talk About

1. Ask:
   - How did the color get into the stem/ leaves/flower? (The important thing about capillarity is that it can make water move up. This is opposite the direction water usually moves, which is down due to gravity. The tiny pieces of water that can get into tiny tubes in the flower are small enough to be drawn upwards by being attracted to the sides of the tubes or capillaries in the stem. The attraction is stronger than the pull of gravity.)

Book to Read (with good ideas for teachers)

How Things Work by Neil Ardley (section on pumps)

Follow-Up Activity

- Use the eyedroppers at the water table to apply paint to create artwork.

Bringing Science Home!
A Note Home to Families About Working With Pumps, Siphons, and Capillary Action

Dear Families,

I asked for some help today and everyone was eager to be of assistance. The children never questioned why the task of moving water from one container to another was necessary. They took pleasure in their work and everyone had their favorite tool. Some tools moved more water than others did. We used spoons, scoops, eyedroppers, and pumps. Ask your child which tool was her or his favorite.

As our bodies did the work to lift the water, the force of gravity helped us by pulling the water down. It's a good thing there is gravity!

Siphoning is fun to do because in moving water this way, the water goes up before it goes down. This amazing way of first using suction and then gravity fascinates children as they try to figure out how it works.

Here is an inexpensive toy that will keep your child entertained for hours (okay, 20 minutes): Plastic eyedroppers (also known as medicine droppers) are wonderful tools that can be purchased at a drugstore. They make every bath a science experience! Just be sure they're plastic and not glass!

Taking Note of Volume

OBJECTIVES

To notice that an empty jar has space inside it and that space is filled with air

To learn that two containers can have different shapes but still hold the same volume

SCIENCE TABLE

Put small cups, a container of water, and short straws on the Science Table. Keep them out for a few weeks, or as long as you are exploring this experience with the children. The children can explore the concept that air has volume by blowing air through the straw onto their hands, filling the cup with water, and using the straw to blow air into the water. (We can see the volume, or shape, of the air as we breathe it out through the straw into the water. The air pushes the water aside.)

TO GET READY—

Exploring Volume

Materials

clear container
water
marker
small stones

What to Do

1. Present the children with a clear container partially filled with water, with the water level marked on the outside of the container. Place a bowl of small stones nearby.

♀ Each science experience has several activities, which, if done in sequence, build on each other.
Doing everything from *To Get Ready* to *Follow-Up Activities* will give children repeated opportunities to understand concepts.
The individual activities can, of course, be used separately, and children often want to repeat their favorite activities.

2. Ask:
   - What is taking up the space inside the container? (air and water)
   - Can we raise the level of water in the container without adding more water or tipping the container?
   - What are some ways we could do that?
3. Have the children try out some of their ideas.
4. If the children don't think of it, suggest putting the stones in the water.

What to Talk About

1. Ask:
   - What is moving the water level?
   - What is taking up the space in the pitcher and filling its volume?

Seeing Air as Bubbles

Materials

2 clear containers—1 large and 1 very small
water
towels

What to Do

1. Fill a large, clear container with water.
   - Hold up an empty, small clear container, such as a baby food jar or medicine bottle.
2. Ask:
   - What is filling the container? (air)
3. Put the small container (open-end first) entirely into the water in the large container.
4. Slowly turn it right side up under the water so air bubbles escape.
5. Repeat this a few times and provide time for all the children to have a turn.
6. All ages love to do this activity but most young preschoolers won't be interested in discussing it.
7. Have plenty of towels ready and/or do this outdoors.

What to Talk About

1. Ask:
   - What is filling the small container? You can invite the children to "blow into it to put your breath in the container," to help them understand that air is filling the container.
   - What came out of it when we turned it over?
   - What are the bubbles made of? (Most things that look empty are full of air. We saw air as it left the bottle and came up through the water. It came out in round shapes—bubbles.)

Air Fills the Container and Keeps the Water Out

Materials

2 clear containers—1 large and 1 very small
tissue
water
towels

What to Do

1. Using the same setup from the previous activity, now put a crumpled bit of tissue in the bottom of the small container (use tape if necessary to hold it in).
2. Repeat the immersion, but this time, do not turn the bottle right side up under water.

What to Talk About

1. Ask:
   - Will the tissue get wet?
   - What is your guess?
   - Why do you think that?
2. After immersing the bottle, pull it out and allow the children to feel the tissue to determine that it is dry. Ask:
   - Why is the tissue dry? (The air took up the volume in the container, and held the water away from the tissue, so the water could not get in to wet the tissue.)
3. Children love to do this activity. Don't be surprised if they don't realize, at first, that the small container needs to be upside down to keep the water out. Give them time to work it out. The younger children may just want to wet the tissue. Children also enjoy mixing the cellulose type of packing peanuts into water and feeling them as they dissolve.

Shape and Volume

Materials

2 cylinders of equal volume but different shape (cut from soda bottles)
dried beans or buttons
small scoop
shallow dish or box lid
removable stickers

What to Do

1. Cut the middle sections from a one-liter soda bottle and a two-liter bottle.
   Note: To tell the two apart, it helps to have one made from a see-through green plastic and one from a clear plastic.
2. Holding one of the cylinders upright, fill it with dried beans. Then pour those same beans into the other cylinder. Mark how high the beans go and cut the excess cylinder off so you have two cylinders of different sizes and shapes, but that hold the same amount of beans.

3. Present these two clear cylinders that are identical in volume but very different in shape (tall and thin, short and wide).

4. Describe the empty space inside each cylinder as volume. Ask the children what is filling the cylinders. (air)

5. Hold the taller, thinner empty cylinder inside a shallow dish and fill it with dried beans.

6. With older children, this can be done with a scoop, counting the scoops to compare the number of scoops that it takes to fill the taller, thinner cylinder with the contents in the shorter, wider cylinder.

What to Talk About

1. Ask:
   - Which cylinder is the biggest? Most children will say the taller one is bigger.

2. Ask:
   - Which one will hold more beans? Have the children record their answers by putting a sticker on the cylinder that they think will hold the most. A few children will think the two volumes will hold an identical amount.

3. Interesting discussions take place when there is a difference of opinion.

Measuring and Comparing the Volumes

Materials
cylinders from previous activity
buttons, teddy bear counters, or any other loose material
small scoop
shallow dish or box lid
stickers

What to Do

1. Fill the shorter cylinder using only the buttons or beans from the first one. This can be done easily by setting the shorter, wider cylinder over and around the taller, thinner cylinder. Then slowly turn the cylinders over, and lift up the taller cylinder to let the buttons slide out the open bottom into the shorter cylinder.

What to Talk About

1. Ask:
   - Do we have too many buttons for this other cylinder to hold?
   - Do we have room for more?
   - Which one can hold more buttons? (Cylinders can be different shapes and still hold the same amount of beans or air or anything. They have the same volume.)

Books to Read
One of Aesop's Fables, "The Crow and the Pitcher" (sometimes called "The Thirsty Crow")
Capacity by Henry Pluckrose
Cook-A-Doodle-Doo! by Janet Stevens and Susan Stevens Crummel
Cubes, Cones, Cylinders & Spheres by Tana Hoban
Solid, Liquid, or Gas? by Fay Robinson

Follow-Up Activities
- Measure the volumes of a variety of containers using sand or water to fill and compare various shapes. Make predictions about which volume is smaller or larger, and then pour back and forth. The idea that the volume of sand (or water) is preserved as it moves from one container to the next seems obvious to adults but not to preschoolers. They may well want "their container" to be the biggest each time.
- Blow bubbles and say, "This small bubble has a small volume of air inside of it. This big bubble has a big volume of air inside of it."

Bringing Science Home!
A Note Home to Families About Taking Note of Volume

Dear Families,

It is an old trick to show someone an empty jar and ask, "What is inside this jar?" Your preschooler is beginning to think about air and notice its existence. Another tough question is, "What are bubbles made of?" When we blow through a straw into a cup of water, is the bubble made of air or water? Or both?

Water, like air, changes shape to fill a space. That makes it a handy substance for comparing the sizes of two containers. One is tall and one is short, but which is bigger? This is an important concept to preschoolers. We had two containers that had different shapes, but held the same amount although one was tall and one was short! The containers have the same capacity to hold water because their volume is the same.

Evaporation and Condensation

OBJECTIVE
To look for signs of evaporation and condensation

SCIENCE TABLE
Put small unbreakable mirrors on the Science Table. Keep them out for a few weeks, or as long as you are exploring this experience with the children. The children can breathe on the mirrors and notice the water condensing. (Be sure to disinfect after use.)

The dress-up mirror is another good place for experimenting with this concept.

TO GET READY—

Exploring Evaporation and Condensation

Materials
paper towels
markers
spray bottle of water

What to Do
1. Encourage each child to draw on a paper towel with markers and then wet it with a spray bottle or a paintbrush.
2. Hang it up to dry.
3. Check at intervals to see if some of the water has left the paper towel (evaporated) so it is drier.

Each science experience has several activities, which, if done in sequence, build on each other.
Doing everything from "To Get Ready" to "Follow-Up Activities" will give children repeated opportunities to understand concepts.
The individual activities can be used separately, and children often want to repeat their favorite activities.

What Happens to Spilled Water?

Materials

water

What to Do

1. Spill a little water on your clothes, making it look like an accident.

What to Talk About

1. Say, "Oops, I spilled water on my clothes! What should I do? Where will the water go?" Some common answers the children will give are "down to the ground," "just stay there" and "into the clothes."
2. Thank the children for their answers, but don't comment on them.

Water on a Blackboard

Materials

container of water
sponge
slate (or blackboard or stone)

What to Do

1. Wipe a slate, a blackboard, or a dark stone with a damp sponge.

What to Talk About

1. Ask:
   - Will the slate stay wet forever?
   - Where will the water go?

   Let's watch and see if that does happen. (We cannot see the water molecules going into the air, but we can see the resulting dryness of the slate.)
2. Begin the next activity, but return to look at the slate in 5-10 minutes.
3. Ask:
   - Has the slate changed?
   - Why is the slate drier now?
   - Where did the water go? (The water from the slate is going into the air in pieces too tiny to see. This is called *evaporation*.)

Meanwhile, Look at Condensation

Materials
thermos of steaming hot water
Plexiglas mirrors
paper towels

What to Do
1. Hold a mirror or your hand over the thermos of steaming water.
   Note: Supervise closely. Water from the tap is usually hot enough.
2. Let each child wipe off some steam from the mirror or feel the dampness of your hand.

What to Talk About
1. Ask:
   - What are you wiping off of the mirror?
   - Where did it come from? (Tiny pieces of water are leaving the thermos and going into the air. This happens to water in puddles and rivers and oceans. It's called evaporation. That evaporated water is landing on the cooler mirror. That's called *condensation*. This happens in clouds.)

Condensing Water

Materials
container of ice cubes and water (use a fresh container for each group)
paper towels

What to Do
1. If the air inside the classroom is too dry, there may not be enough water in the air to condense on the container of ice water. Be sure to try this activity yourself before having the children try it.

2. Put out a container filled with water and lots of ice.

What to Talk About
1. Feel the outside of this container.
2. Ask:
   - Is it dry, damp, or really wet?
3. Check it again in a few minutes to see if there has been a change.
4. Ask:
   - Why is the outside wet?
   - Where did the water come from? (Water is in the air. When the warm water in the air touches the cold bottle it collects on the bottle, little by little, until there is enough to make drops. This is called condensation.)

Feel Water Evaporating From Our Skin

Materials
none needed

What to Do
1. Encourage the children to wipe a wet finger across their bare forearm or lick their arm, then blow on the area.

What to Talk About
1. Ask:
   - How does it feel?
   - Why do you think it feels that way? (The coolness is the warmth going away from your body. The warmth goes away with the tiny pieces of water that are going into the air. Your body warms the water, and then tiny pieces of water go into the air, taking the warmth with them. Evaporation is cooling your arm.)

Condensing the Water in Our Breath

Materials

Plexiglas mirrors
paper towels
bleach solution spray
towel

What to Do

1. Have each child breathe on a Plexiglas mirror. (Clean after each group with bleach solution spray.)

What to Talk About

1. Ask:
   - What do you see?
   - What is happening? (Putting warm breath on the cooler mirror makes the warm water in the breath of air collect on the mirror. This is called *condensation*.)

Sing About Condensation

Materials

none needed

What to Do

1. Sing the following to the tune of "Three Blind Mice."

   Condensation, condensation,
   Water in the air, water in the air.
   It floats around until it's chilled,
   On a cool mirror or colder still,
   An icy drink and moist air will
   Make condensation, drops of condensation.

Book to Read

Down Comes the Rain by Franklyn M. Branley has nice drawings, and is a good, comprehensive explanation of how evaporation and condensation work in the rain cycle for teachers and older preschoolers.

Follow-Up Activity

- Put the same small amount of water into each of two clear plastic cups or jars. Have the children mark the level of the water on the outside of the jar with a line drawn on tape. Cover one jar with plastic wrap. Check every day to see if there is still the same amount of water in each jar. (The cover will keep the water in the covered jar while the water in the uncovered jar evaporates.)

Bringing Science Home!
A Note Home to Families About Evaporation and Condensation

Dear Families,

How do we explain something we can't see? We can't see water particles as evaporation carries them into the air, but we can see signs of evaporation and condensation.

The children began to learn about evaporation and condensation by watching hot, steaming water rise from a thermos into the air and disappear. Holding our hands over the steam made our hands wet, so we could feel the effects of water evaporating.

Have you ever compared how wet skin feels compared to dry skin? The children noticed how cold their wet skin felt. The coolness is created when the warmth leaves their bodies. The warmth goes away with the tiny pieces of water that are going into the air. Their bodies warm the water, and then tiny pieces of water go into the air, taking the warmth with them. Evaporation was cooling their arms.

Drawing condensation pictures is fun. All you need is a mirror or windowpane and your breath. Putting warm breath on the cooler mirror makes the warm water in the breath of air collect on the mirror. Then you can draw in the condensation with your finger.

Sound Is Vibration

OBJECTIVE
To feel sound

SCIENCE TABLE
Materials

6 small containers, such as film canisters
assorted materials, such as cotton balls, pennies,
    rice, or bells
glue
tape
index cards
markers

What to Do

1. Fill pairs (6 containers total) with the same material such as cotton balls, pennies, rice, or bells and seal them. Plastic eggs also work, but use all the same color to keep the children from using color as a cue.
2. Tape a sample of the objects in each pair of containers.
3. Ask the children to shake the containers to find the pairs that have the same materials (make the same sound).
4. Then the children put the matching card in front of the pair of containers.
5. Add new pairs of containers, as needed.
6. Put them out on the Science Table. Keep them out for a few weeks, or as long as you are exploring this experience with the children.

Each science experience has several activities, which, if done in sequence, build on each other. Doing everything from "To Get Ready" to "Follow-Up Activities" will give children repeated opportunities to understand concepts. The individual activities can be used separately, and children often want to repeat their favorite activities.

Exploring Sound

Materials
paper and pen

What to Do
1. Play a "Stop and Listen" game outside.
2. Tell the children that every few minutes you will give the prearranged signal for everyone to stop and listen to the sounds they hear.
3. Suggest they listen for the loudest/softest/strangest/closest sound.
4. Make a list of the sounds that they hear.

Feel Your Throat Vibrating

Materials
none needed

What to Do
1. Put your hand on your throat while talking and encourage the children to do the same.

What to Talk About
1. Say your name while you touch your throat. Ask:
   - What do you feel? (The movement of our throats is called a vibration, which is small, fast movements over and over.)
   - Can you make your throat vibrate without making a sound? (No.)
2. After each of the following activities, ask:
   - What do you feel?
   - What do you notice?
   - What part of the instrument is vibrating?
   - How is the sound made?

- How does the sound get to our ears?
- Is sound the same thing as vibration?

Feel a Triangle Vibrate

Materials
triangle musical instrument

What to Do
1. Strike a triangle and let each child feel the vibration with one finger.

4. Demonstrate how to play the single-string can instrument.
5. Loop the end of the string around your foot, hold the can up high enough to keep the string taut, and pluck!
6. Encourage the children to try the instrument.
7. Now encourage the children to pluck a string (not attached to a can) held between your hands. Compare the sounds.

Make Music With Vibration

Materials

small boxes (1/2-gallon juice or milk carton)
scissors
rubber bands

What to Do

1. Make guitars out of small boxes and rubber bands. Milk cartons work well.
2. Pre-cut a large oval hole on one side.
3. Stretch three rubber bands around the box the long way, across the opening. The sound will be better if the rubber bands can be suspended above the box a bit by slightly crushing in the side with the hole and leaving the end edges up to act like a bridge on a guitar, violin, or other stringed instrument.
4. Ask the children to join you in playing a familiar song such as "Old MacDonald Had a Farm," or any other well-known tune.

2. Then let children stop the sound/vibration by grabbing the triangle with their hand.

See and Feel a String Vibrate

Materials

cans
hammer and nail (adult only)
string
scissors

What to Do

1. Make a string-can instrument by punching a hole in the center of the bottom of a can of any size (adult only) with a hammer and nail.
2. Put the end of a 4-foot length of string through the hole, knot it from the inside, and make a loop big enough for your foot on the other end.
3. This is similar to a single-string bass.

What to Talk About

1. Ask:
   - Can you feel the vibration?
   - How does the kazoo change the sound you made with your body?

Make a Musical Instrument to Take Home

Materials

1 cardboard (toilet paper) tube for each child
wax paper squares
rubber bands

What to Do

1. Make a musical instrument called a kazoo.
2. The children will be eager to make one after they use one finger to feel the vibration of the wax paper on yours as you say their names.
3. Wrap a square of wax paper over one end of a toilet paper tube and secure with a rubber band.
4. Teach the children not to blow, but to hum or talk into the tube with their mouths very close to, but not pressing on, the tube. An easy sound to start with is "toot, toot, toot." They may blow anyway and discover that they can blow off the wax paper cover. No harm done, eventually they'll get back to making sound.

Books to Read

And the Cow Said "Moo!" by Mildred Phillips
Listen to the Desert/Oye al Deserto by Pat Mora
Marsh Music by Marianne Collins Berkes
Slop Goes the Soup: A Noisy Warthogs Word Book by Pamela Duncan
Sounds All Around by Wendy Pfeffer

Follow-Up Activity

- Make "telephones" out of two paper cups/tin cans/juice cans and a 10-foot length of string. Poke a tiny hole in the bottom of each container and put the string through the hole from the outside to the inside. Knot the end of the string on the inside, large enough to keep it from pulling through. To operate, two people each hold a container and stand far enough apart to keep the string taut. One person holds the container to their ear while the other speaks quietly enough into the other container (keeping the string taut) that they cannot be easily heard without the "telephone."

Bringing Science Home!
A Note Home to Families About Sound Is Vibration

Dear Families,

What does all sound have in common? Feel the answer by putting your hand on your throat while you talk. What do you feel? The movement of our throats is called vibration (small movements over and over, very fast). Can you make your throat vibrate without making a sound?

Today, we made a musical instrument to bring home. It is called a "kazoo." We made it by covering one end of a cardboard tube with wax paper. When you talk or sing into the open end of the tube, your voice has a funny sound. The buzzing quality to the sound is made when the wax paper vibrates. Touch it gently with one finger to "feel" sound.

Making a Chemical Reaction to Create Slime

OBJECTIVES
To observe how substances change when mixed together

To notice if a substance flows, drips, or maintains its shape when we pour it

SCIENCE TABLE

Materials

3 small, clear jars

playdough, slime (see recipe on page 173), and white glue

glue and tape

What to Do

1. Put ½ cup of one of the following—playdough, slime, and white glue separately—into separate small, clear jars.
2. Tightly seal the tops onto the jars.
3. Place the jars on the Science Table.
4. The children explore what happens to each substance when they tip and shake the jars and then let the jars sit still. Does the substance flow, drip, or maintain its shape?
5. Keep the jars out for a few weeks, or as long as you are exploring this experience with the children.

TO GET READY—
Exploring Mixtures Independently

Materials

yogurt cups

liquids, such as vinegar, water, food coloring, and white glue

solids, such as flour, baking soda, cornstarch, and salt

pump bottles, optional

small scoops or measuring spoons

index cards

markers

spoons for mixing

♀ Each science experience has several activities, which, if done in sequence, build on each other. Doing everything from "To Get Ready" to "Follow-Up Activities" will give children repeated opportunities to understand concepts. The individual activities can be used separately, and children often want to repeat their favorite activities.

What to Do

1. Talk about how we follow recipes to make mixtures such as cake batter or paints. Recipes tell us what ingredients or materials to use, how much to use, and in what order to add them.

2. More experimenting will happen if the teacher accepts that this is a very messy project (but it is worth it). Cleanup is easier if a layer of newspapers is put down before beginning the mixing.

3. Encourage the children to make mixtures in the classroom, or outside, using liquids such as water, juice, milk, vinegar, food coloring, and white glue, and solids such as flour, sugar, baking soda, cornstarch, and salt.

4. Give the children small containers such as yogurt cups in which to mix their chosen ingredients.

5. Liquids such as vinegar can be dispensed with little mess if the children can help themselves from a pump bottle such as those used for liquid soap.

6. Make small scoops or measuring spoons available to limit the mess while measuring the solid ingredients.

7. Have the children record their first mixture as a recipe on an index card using agreed-upon standard pictures to represent each of the ingredients, such as a square of blue for water, large spoon for a tablespoon measure, or a "squirt" shape for liquid from a pump.

Examining the Ingredients—Are They Liquids or Solids?

Materials

Borax (a laundry booster that can be found in the detergent aisle of grocery stores)
liquid white glue
water
bowls
chart paper and markers, optional

What to Do

1. Pour white glue, Borax, and water in separate bowls.
2. Show the children the raw materials of the activity—white glue, Borax and water, each in a separate bowl.

What to Talk About

1. For each material, ask the children to decide if it is a liquid (water), solid (sand), or a gas (like air), and discuss some of the substances' characteristics (dry, wet, sticky, clear, white, thick).
2. Ask:
   - Does the substance flow, drip, or maintain its shape?
3. If desired, record descriptions of each of the three substances on a chart, leaving a fourth space for describing the new mixture you will make.

Measuring to Make a Solution

Materials

water
Borax (a laundry booster that can be found on the detergent aisle)
large, clear plastic jar with a tight-fitting lid
Mr. Yuk sticker (the symbol for poison: an unhappy face with the tongue sticking out)

What to Do

1. Help the children measure 1 cup of water into an unbreakable, clear container with a lid. This will make enough solution for a class of 12 children.
2. Mix 1 tablespoon of Borax into the water, close the container, and shake until the Borax is mostly dissolved.
3. Label this jar with a Mr. Yuk sticker, or other clear symbol that this solution is not to drink!

What to Talk About

1. Ask:
   - What do you think will happen if we mix the Borax into the water? (We are mixing a solid into a liquid.)
   - What do you see happening? (When a solid is dissolved into a liquid, we call the resulting mixture a solution.)
2. We will use this solution in our experiment. The Borax solution is safe to touch but not to drink or get into our eyes. It would sting. (Also make note that it is poisonous.)

Mixing the Two Liquid Ingredients

Materials

craft sticks or spoons   liquid white glue
small paper cups   water

What to Do

1. Give each child a craft stick and a small paper cup containing 1 tablespoon of white glue.
2. Help them add 1 tablespoon of water and mix thoroughly.

What to Talk About

1. Tell the children to stir immediately and keep stirring.
2. Ask:
   - What is in your cup? (Glue)
   - What do you think will happen when we add some water to the glue? Let's find out! Tell me if you think the glue has changed. (Many children say they have made milk. Ask them to smell it.)
   - Does it smell like milk?
   Describe the way it looks and smells.

Adding the Solution

Materials

Borax-water solution
glue-water solution in small cups
craft sticks or spoons

What to Do

1. Help the children add 1 tablespoon of the Borax-water solution to the glue-water mixture in their cup.

What to Talk About

1. Tell the children to stir immediately and keep stirring.
2. Ask:
   - What do you think will happen when we add some Borax solution to the glue and water mixture in your cup? Let's find out! Tell me if you see a change. (The children will be very excited when the Borax solidifies the glue mixture into a stiff slime.)
   - What is happening to the mixture? Describe the way it looks, feels, and smells.
3. Record the description on the chart describing the ingredients.
4. Ask:
   - Why do you think the mixture changed?

Feeling the Slime

Materials

mixture from previous activity
markers, optional
towels
resealable plastic bags
information sheet for parents (see Bringing Science Home! page 173)

What to Do

1. When the children have completely mixed the ingredients together, let them knead the slimy mixture in their hands or on the tabletop.
2. The more it is handled, the drier it becomes.
3. It can be colored by drawing on it with washable markers, a wonderful extension to the activity.
4. Store the slime in a resealable plastic bag and send it home with the information sheet for the parents taped to the outside.

Make sure the bags are sealed because although the slime feels somewhat solid, it will flow and will stick to anything that is not hard.

What to Talk About

1. Ask:
   - What does your slime feel like?
   - What can it do?
   - Is it a liquid similar to water, or a solid such as a block? (Children soon find out that it can stretch, bounce, be pulled apart, and put back together.)
2. Talk about not putting the slime in your mouths. The slime is safe to touch and play with but would give you a stomachache if you ate it.

Books to Read

Kids' Crazy Art Concoctions: 50 Mysterious Mixtures for Art and Craft Fun by Jill Frankel Hauser
Mudpies and Other Recipes: A Cookbook for Dolls by Marjorie Winslow
Pancakes for Breakfast by Tomie dePaola
The Piggy in the Puddle by Charlotte Pomerante
Pretend Soup and Other Real Recipes: A Cookbook for Preschoolers and Up by Mollie Katzen and Ann L. Henderson

Follow-Up Activity

- Cook something to eat for snack following a simple recipe, written in symbols if possible. A good one for the youngest children is making colored applesauce. Each child can decide which color of food coloring to stir into a small cup of applesauce.

Bringing Science Home!
A Note Home to Families About Making a Chemical Reaction to Create Slime

Dear Families,

This is a note about the "slime" in your child's bag. It's safe, it's icky, and it's made from white glue mixed with a borax-and-water solution!

Borax is a naturally occurring mineral that is sold as a laundry booster (some people use it for washing diapers). If your child gets slime on their hands and then rubs their eyes or licks their fingers, it's safe. If they eat it, they may get a stomachache, but you don't need to call poison control. To wash out of clothing, just wash as usual.

RECIPE FOR SLIME
Materials
Borax (a laundry booster that is found in the detergent aisle of grocery stores)
water
paper cups
measuring spoons
1 tablespoon white glue
spoons for stirring

1. *Mix one tablespoon of Borax into 1 cup water and stir until dissolved, and set aside.*
2. *In a separate cup, mix 1 tablespoon water with 1 tablespoon white school glue and stir until thoroughly combined.*
3. *Now add 1 tablespoon of the borax-and-water solution to the glue and water mixture and stir until "slimed."*

***Safety precautions:** An adult should mix the Borax solution and put a lid on it while it is not being used to keep it out of eyes and mouths. If it does get in the eyes, rinse gently with running water.*

Eating Sunlight

OBJECTIVE
To make the connection between the sun's energy and life on Earth

SCIENCE TABLE
Materials
large tray
potting soil
grass seeds
small plastic farm animals

What to Do

1. *Fill a 9" x 13" (or larger) tray with potting soil.*
2. *Plant grass seed and water it.*
3. *When the grass has grown, ask the children to set it up as they imagine a farm would look.*
4. *Provide small toy animals and people, twigs from outside for building, and a small jar lid for a pond. Add other small plants to represent crops and trees.*
5. *Put this on the Science Table and keep it out for a few weeks, or as long as you are exploring this experience with the children.*

TO GET READY—
Exploring Sunlight

Materials
2 shallow containers
potting soil
grass seeds

What to Do

1. Experiment with growing grass.
2. Fill two containers with potting soil.
3. Plant grass seeds in each container.
4. Put one container in the sunlight and the other in darkness (covered up by a large overturned can or in a closet).
5. Look at the grass every day to check for growth and to add water to both containers if necessary.
6. Grass takes about a week to grow, so you may want to do this activity a week or two before you introduce this science unit on sunlight.

Each science experience has several activities, which, if done in sequence, build on each other.
Doing everything from "To Get Ready" to "Follow-Up Activities" will give children repeated opportunities to understand concepts.
The individual activities can be used separately, and children often want to repeat their favorite activities.

3. Put the object on the paper, cover with a Plexiglas sheet to hold the paper in place and put it under the classroom light, not the light coming in the window. (A clear sheet of plastic wrap also works to keep the paper in place, but it is much more difficult to move.)
4. Wait 20 minutes or more before stopping the reaction by washing the paper.
5. Label it as the "indoor print" so it can be compared to ones made outdoors later.
6. This also gives you practice making the sun prints. When you make them later outside in the direct sunshine, you will have to move quickly to make a clear print because the strong sunlight will react quickly with the paper.

What to Talk About

1. Ask:
   - ♀ Does the grass look the same in both containers?
   - ♀ Which one is healthier?
   - ♀ Which one is growing the best?
2. Save these grass pots for continued discussion on eating sunlight.

Make a Sun Print Indoors

Materials
sunlight-reactive paper
flat objects
Plexiglas sheet

What to Do
1. A day or week before introducing this science unit on sunlight, make a "sun print" indoors using sunlight-reactive paper.
2. Choose a flat object, such as a shape cut from foil or paper.

Explore Sunlight

Materials
none needed

What to Do
1. Go outdoors on a sunny day.
2. Try tasting, smelling, and listening to sunlight.

What to Talk About
1. Ask:
   - How can we sense sunlight?
   - Can we taste it?
   - Can we hear it?
   - Can we smell it? (We can feel it.)
   - What happens if we get a lot of sunshine on our skin? (Sunlight is light and another kind of energy called ultraviolet radiation. Our skin turns darker to protect our inside layers from this energy.)

Make a Sun Print Outdoors

Materials
sunlight-reactive paper
Plexiglas sheet
flat leaves or plant parts
a pan to hold water
water
2 small containers of dirt planted with grass seed
large can
plastic toy cow

What to Do
1. Show example of a "sun print," silhouettes made on sunlight-reactive paper.
2. Have each child gather a few flat leaves or other fairly flat plant parts to make sun prints using light reactive paper. Small objects from the classroom may be used instead.
3. When the children have their leaves, help them quickly set up their "sun print." You must work quickly so that through exposure, the sun does not change the color of the entire sheet, but just the part of the paper that is not covered by the plants.
4. The blue side of the paper faces upward, the plant parts go on top.
5. Cover with a sheet of Plexiglas to keep everything from blowing away while the print develops.

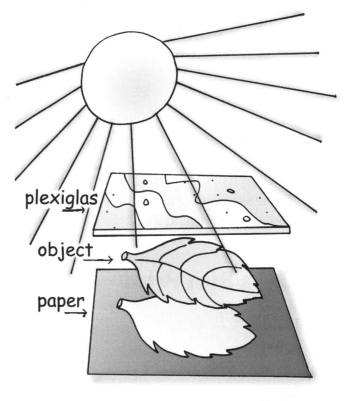

6. It will take about five minutes for the silhouette to form. While you are waiting, move into the shade and read a short book.
7. Sometimes the children will remember which print is theirs, but you could also write each child's name on a sticker ahead of time to put on their paper just before they set up their print.
8. Rinse the "sun prints" in water to stop the chemical process.

What to Talk About

1. Ask:
   - What do you think will happen to the paper in the sun? (The color of this paper can be changed by the sun's energy, the same as our skin can get a suntan.)
   - Has the paper changed color? (The places on the paper that were in shadow or covered up by the leaves are white, and the rest is blue. The sun's energy made the paper change color.)
2. Compare this sun print to the one that the children did inside the classroom.

Read While the Sun Does Its Work

Materials

book about sunlight, such as:
   The Sun Is My Favorite Star by Frank Asch
   The Way to Start a Day by Byrd Baylor

What to Do

1. Move out of the sun to read aloud while waiting for the paper to react to sunlight.

What to Talk About

1. Ask:
   - What do plants need to grow?
   - Where do they get it?
   - What do we need to grow and where do we get it? (Plants need water, sunlight, and the minerals in dirt. We need water and food. We need to eat plants or animals that ate plants).
   - What would our world be like without a sun?

Talk About the Grass Again

Materials

2 grass beds from "To Get Ready—Exploring Sunlight"
plastic toy cows

What to Do

1. Look at the two grass beds grown last week.

What to Talk About

1. Ask:
   - Is there a difference between the two grass beds?
   - Why is the one that was hidden from the sun so pale? (The grass growing that was hidden from the sun will be pale green since it is unable to make food for itself without sunlight.)
   - Which one would a cow rather eat?
2. Ask each child to put a plastic cow in the grass plot they think the cow would prefer as they make their decision.
3. Talk about how plants need the sun's energy to grow well.

Churn Butter

Materials

1 pint of whipping cream
plastic jar with tight-fitting lid
crackers

What to Do

1. Make butter to help the children make the connection between the sun's energy and our life on earth. Explain to the children that the grass uses the sun's energy to grow, the cow eats the grass to grow, and we eat the butter to grow. When we eat butter, we eat the sun's energy.
2. Pour 1 pint of room-temperature whipping cream into a jar with a tight-fitting lid.
3. Have the children take turns shaking the jar for 20 to 30 minutes until the butter forms a ball.
4. Pour out the watery whey and spread the butter on crackers. Enjoy!

What to Talk About

1. Ask:
   - Who made the butter? (We did, from the cow's milk.)
   - How did the cow get the energy to make milk? (From the grass.)
   - How did the grass get the energy to grow? (From the water, the sun, and the soil. The grass uses the sun's energy to grow, the cow eats the grass to grow, the cow makes milk, and we drink the cow's milk or use it to make butter.)
   - What would our world be like without a sun?

Books to Read

Bread Is for Eating by David and Phillis Gershator
Counting Cows by Woody Jackson
Little Green Thumbs by Mary An Van Hage, et al
The Milk Makers by Gail Gibbons
Sun Bread by Elisa Kleven
The Sun Is My Favorite Star by Frank Asch

Bringing Science Home!
A Note Home to Families About Eating Sunlight

Dear Families,

When the sun shines on green plants, the plants can make food with the sun's energy. Then we can eat the plants, which is our way of eating the sun's energy! We are learning about sunlight by making "sun prints" using a special paper that changes when you put it where the sun's energy, or light, can shine on it. Do we need the sun's energy to grow?

We talked about how the sun's energy helps the grass grow, and the grass helps the cow grow, and the cow's milk helps people grow. Then we shook some cow's cream to make butter. Yummy!

Objects in Motion

TO GET READY—

Exploring Objects in Motion

Make a mobile or stabile using Alexander Calder's art as inspiration.

Alexander Calder was an artist whose moving sculptures were named mobiles.

Mobiles are made of objects of various sizes and shapes hanging in balance from a central object, often a stiff piece of wire. Art foam and wire can be cut, twisted, and attached together to make a hanging, moving sculpture—a mobile!

OBJECTIVES

To experience the way various objects move in a variety of focused situations
To provide the opportunity to predict and think about the movement of objects

SCIENCE TABLE

Put the following items on the Science Table. Keep them out for a few weeks, or as long as you are exploring this experience with the children.

- *Newton's Cradle (see pages 182-183)—be prepared to untangle it frequently*
- *a small ramp*
- *variety of objects to roll or slide down the ramp*

Tell a Ball to Move

Materials

soft, foam ball

What to Do

1. Sit in a circle on the floor.
2. Tell the children that you are going to try to move a sponge ball across the circle by setting it in front of you and telling it to roll.

Each science experience has several activities, which, if done in sequence, build on each other.
Doing everything from "To Get Ready" to "Follow-Up Activities" will give children repeated opportunities to understand concepts.
The individual activities can be used separately, and children often want to repeat their favorite activities.

What to Talk About

1. Say, "Move, ball. Go across the circle. It's not moving! Why isn't the ball moving? What do I need to do?"
2. The children will readily tell or show you that the ball must be pushed or rolled or thrown before it will move.

Move the Ball

Materials
soft, foam ball

What to Do

1. Send the ball rolling by tapping it gently.
2. Make sure each child gets a turn rolling the ball.

What to Talk About

1. Say, "So that's how to get the ball to move!"
2. Ask:
   - What is making the ball move? (The force of our tapping it makes it move. The ball will not move unless a force acts on it. Sir Isaac Newton was a scientist who lived a long time ago and named this piece of information one of the natural laws of physics, the law of inertia. Everyone knows the ball won't move unless you put some force on it but he was the first one to describe it and to say it happens every time.)

Put the Attention on Gravity

Materials
soft, foam ball

What to Do

1. Hold the ball between your palms, on the floor in front of you.
2. Pull your hands away (to show that the ball will not move.)
3. Next, hold the ball in the air between your palms.
4. Drop it by just letting go, pulling your hands back to show that you did not throw the ball down.

What to Talk About

1. Say, "I did not push or throw the ball down. I did not use force; I just moved my hands away. Why did it move down to the floor?" (Gravity is a force that acts on everything on our earth.)
2. Say, "You have seen examples of how gravity affects objects. Can you tell me what the natural law of gravity might be? What are the rules for gravity?" (Gravity is a force, just like your tap on the ball. It pulls everything towards the ground. The children's answers might not be entirely true, but do not correct them unless they ask you to. Encouraging them to hypothesize is more important than learning the correct definition of "gravity." They will have many other opportunities in school to learn definitions.)

Relate Gravity to Car Seat Safety

Materials
several clear plastic cups
several marbles

What to Do
1. Tell the children that the clear plastic cup is your car, the marble is you, and that you are going for a drive.
2. Put the marble inside the clear plastic cup.
3. Holding the cup on its side, push the cup forward slowly across the floor and then slowly stop it. Then go out for another "drive," this time stopping suddenly to avoid another "car."
4. Encourage the children to try it.

What to Talk About
1. Ask:
   - What force is making the cup move?
   - What force is making the marble move?
   - What stopped the cup? (The force of my hand, holding it still.)
   - What happens if another "car" bumps into me?
   - Did the marble stop with the cup? Why not?
   - In real life, how do we make sure that we don't keep going when our cars stop?
   - What holds us in the car? (Our seatbelts and our car seats. Some children may point out that having the doors closed helps keep us in the car.)

Put on a Seat Belt

Materials
several clear plastic cups
several marbles
masking tape

What to Do
1. Put a piece of masking tape across the marble that is still inside the cup.
2. Move and stop the cup.
3. Have all the children try it.

What to Talk About
1. Say, "This tape is my seat belt. Do you think it will hold me in? Let's try it."

Make a Newton's Cradle

Materials
3 golf balls or ping-pong balls
dowel or long, strong cardboard tube
drill or other tool to make holes
eye screws
string
scissors

What to Do

1. Make this simplified version of a Newton's Cradle, a contraption to teach about natural laws of physics through play.
2. Drill or make a hole in each ball and insert an eye screw into each one.
3. Cut three equal lengths of string, about 3 feet.
4. Tie each string in a loop through an eye screw in each ball.
5. Tape the top of each loop onto the dowel or cardboard tube, maintaining the proper distance between the balls (just far apart enough that the balls rest side by side just barely touching).
6. Hang between two chairs. Shorten or lengthen the loops as needed.
7. Show the children this contraption.
8. Hold one of the end balls up at the dowel level and as far away as the string will allow.

Test the Hypotheses

Materials

Newton's Cradle (see previous activity)

What to Do

1. Drop the ball.
2. Now that the children have focused their attention on making a hypothesis, it's their turn to play with the balls.

What to Talk About

1. Ask:
   - Did the ball fall the way you thought it would? (The forces of gravity made it move down.)
   - Did the other balls move? (The middle ball did not move very much even though the raised ball hit it).

What to Talk About

1. Ask:
   - What will happen when I lift up this one on the end and then let it go? (Demonstrate how you will lift it up but don't let go until they give their hypotheses.)
   - Will the other balls move? Let's see.

   - What was the force that made them move? (The force of gravity changed into the force of a tap when it passed from the falling ball into the middle ball and moved the third ball.)

Books to Read

101 Science Poems & Songs tor Young Learners (see poem "Gravity") by Meish Goldish

Calder: 1898-1976 (Album Series) by Jacob Baal-Teshuva and Alexander Calder

Isaac Newton and Gravity by Steve Parker

The Science Book of Gravity by Neil Ardley

Wheel Away by Dayle Ann Dodds

Follow-Up Activities

° Play with a marble drop, a series of chutes for a marble to race in. Make your own marble drop using cardboard tubes, some whole, some cut lengthwise in half. Tape the various tubes to a stiff cardboard sheet in such a way as to direct the fall of a marble dropped into the top tube into the next tube and then the next, all the way to the bottom. Tape some of the tubes at a gentle slope. By using one of those cardboard tri-fold stands commonly used in science fairs as the support, you can make a self-supporting marble drop.

° Make paper airplanes and blow bubbles. Talk about how they move.

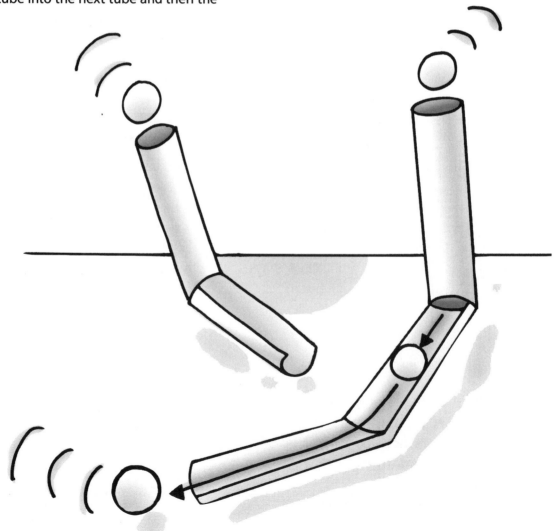

Bringing Science Home!
A Note Home to Families About Objects in Motion

Dear Families,

Everyone knows a ball won't move unless you force it in some way. To get it to move we must throw or kick it. Sir Isaac Newton was a scientist who lived a long time ago and named this piece of information one of the natural laws of physics, the law of inertia. Everyone knew about it; he was just the first one to describe it.

We can also let gravity help—we just let go and the ball moves to the ground. We call it "falling." What would games be like without the force of gravity?

Our Sense of Touch

TO GET READY—

Exploring Our Sense of Touch With a "Feely Box"

Materials

box
scissors
old socks
glue gun (adult only), or tape and staples

What to Do

1. Make a "Feely Box" with any size box.
2. Cut round holes in two sides of the box, large enough for an adult hand.
3. Attach the tops of old socks to the holes (using a glue gun, or tape and staples). These will act as "tunnels" for hands to reach inside the box while still keeping the objects inside hidden. The children can touch the objects without seeing them, making full use of their sense of touch.

OBJECTIVE

To experience our sense of touch and to notice its limitations

SCIENCE TABLE

Keep the Feely Box (at right) in the classroom for a week or two. Using two sizes of the same object such as square blocks or counting bears, the children can play "Find the Big One, Find the Small One," using only their sense of touch to find the larger or the smaller of the two sizes. For older children or ones with experience, add medium-sized objects to the box.

Each science experience has several activities, which, if done in sequence, build on each other.
Doing everything from "To Get Ready" to "Follow-Up Activities" will give children repeated opportunities to understand concepts.
The individual activities can, of course, be used separately, and children often want to repeat their favorite activities.

4. For children who are fearful, a removable lid allows the objects to be easily viewed (and changed).

5. Ask the children to bring objects to put into the "Feely Box."

6. While the children are not looking, put one or many objects inside the box. Invite them to reach inside and describe the feeling of an object, but not say the name of the object.

7. Can other children guess the name?

Feeling Sensations

Materials

warm and cold discovery objects
light and heavy discovery objects
smooth and rough discovery objects

What to Do

1. Have a variety of objects available to experience different sensations: warm and cold (warm and cold water, or a hot water bottle and an ice pack), light and heavy (feathers or Styrofoam blocks and stones), and smooth and rough (the two sides of a piece of sandpaper).

What to Talk About

1. Say, "Let's feel these things. Which one do you want to touch? What does that feel like?" (Children often will name the object, "a rock," without naming the sensation.) You may need to say, "And how does your rock feel? Mine feels rough and bumpy, and it is heavy." (We use our sense of touch to find out about our world. We can feel the difference between different textures, weights, and temperatures.)

2. Use these objects in the Feely Box.

A Sensitive Game

Materials

cardboard
scissors
water-soluble marker
a sensitive plant (Mimosa pudica) (see "Follow-Up Activities" page 188)

What to Do

1. Play a game to test how sensitive our skin is. The challenge is to locate the spot on your arm that was touched by a marker using only your sense of touch. (Four- and five-year-old children enjoy this game if being "right" is not emphasized; younger children may not find it interesting.)

2. Make a large cardboard shield to put in front of the face and body, with two arches cut from the bottom edge to put the arms through. The shield is preferable to a blindfold for many children.

3. Ask one child to be first, or demonstrate the game on yourself.

4. Place the shield on a child's lap with his arms poking through, or use a blindfold.

5. Touch the back of the child's forearm gently with the tip of a water-soluble marker.

6. Ask the child, with the shield still in place, to find that spot with one finger, without peeking.

7. Lift the shield so he can see how close he was to the actual spot.

8. Now have this same child help you try it, so he can see that even grownups can fail to find the touched spot when not looking.

9. Repeat with a dot to the palm of hand. If there is time, try a spot on the neck, cheek, or back of the hand.

10. Notice if it is easier to identify the marked spot on certain parts of our bodies.

What to Talk About

1. Ask:
   - Is it easier to find the marker dot on our arm or on our palm? (Our skin is called "sensitive" where it can feel small touches.)

Sensitive Plants Feel Our Touch

Materials

a sensitive plant, such as Mimosa pudica

What to Do

1. Use a sensitive plant, such as Mimosa pudica, to demonstrate how some plants react to our touch.

What to Talk About

1. When someone tickles our foot, we pull it away because we feel the funny touch. If you tickle a plant, will it pull away? A few plants are able to move when touched.

Books to Read

Feely Bugs: To Touch and Feel by David A. Carter
Looking Out for Sarah by Glenna Lang
My Five Senses by Aliki
Pat the Bunny by Dorothy Kunhardt
Seven Blind Mice by Ed Young
Touch (Explore Your Senses) by Laurence P. Pringle

Follow-Up Activities

- Plant seeds of a sensitive plant (Mimosa pudica) to grow in the classroom. The seedlings will be ready to touch in about one month, but will do best if touched only once a day. Seeds can be ordered from Thompson and Morgan Ltd. at 800-274-7333.

- Make collages that you can touch, using fabrics with a variety of textures, sand, sticks, sandpaper, and other interesting textured materials.

Bringing Science Home!
A Note Home to Families About Our Sense of Touch

Dear Families,

The largest organ of the human body is the skin. The children have been exploring their sense of touch by touching objects that are warm, flat, smooth, wet, rough, cold, furry, dry, squishy, and soft.

It's fun to play a guessing game to test our sense of touch. Ask your child to put a small object inside a paper bag without you seeing it. Then put your hand in and try to guess what is inside. Use your words to describe what you are feeling before you name it. Then it's your child's turn!

Mixing and Separating Colors

OBJECTIVES
To explore combining and separating color
To notice if the same results are achieved each time the same two colors are combined
Note: *The children do not need to be able to identify the color name correctly to participate in the activities.*

SCIENCE TABLE
Put squares of colored acetate or florist's plastic on the Science Table. Keep them out for a few weeks, or as long as you are exploring this experience with the children.

TO GET READY—

Exploring Mixing and Separating Colors

Read a book about colors (see suggestions on page 192). Use color names in casual conversation.

Mix Colors Using Plastic Squares

Materials
squares of red, blue, and yellow florist's plastic or
    acetate
white paper sheets

What to Do
1. Let each child play with squares of red, yellow, and blue florist's plastic or acetate using a sheet of white paper as the background.
   Note: The plastic or acetate can be purchased from craft or artist stores, or from party stores as wrapping paper.

What to Talk About
1. Ask:
   - What happens when the colors come together and overlap?
   - Does it always make the same new color?
   Let's do it again and see.

♀ Each science experience has several activities, which, if done in sequence, build on each other.
Doing everything from "To Get Ready" to "Follow-Up Activities" will give children repeated opportunities to understand concepts.
The individual activities can be used separately, and children often want to repeat their favorite activities.

- When another child overlaps the same colors, does it make the same new color? (We are mixing the colors. If the red is dark enough, overlapping all three colors will make a color that is almost black. We can mix and separate all three colors.)
- Show me your green color. (Some children will say, "I didn't get a green." Ask them if they can make one.)

Spin a Top to Mix Colors

Materials
tops, purchased or made

What to Do
1. To make the top, glue colored tissue paper to a purchased top, covering each third of the "pie" with red, yellow, or blue tissue paper. Inexpensive plastic tops can be purchased at party stores, or you can make one using a two-inch cardboard circle as the body and a short stick as the stem.
2. Show the children a top that is colored in thirds, each pie-shaped section a different color.
3. Ask them if there is one color or more on the top.

4. Spin the top and watch the colors mix. (Spinning a top is difficult for young children but encourage them to try it.)

What to Talk About
1. Ask:
   - What do you see happening to the colors? (The colors look like they change but when the top stops, they are still there.)
   - Why do you think that is? (The colors can be mixed and separated.)

The Color Black Can Be Separated

Materials
white coffee filters
washable black marker
clear, flat-bottomed container
water
clothespins

What to Do
1. Show the children a black washable marker.
2. Ask them what color the marker is.
3. Ask each child to dot a coffee filter with the marker or draw some lines on the filter.
4. Put an inch of water in a clear, flat-bottomed container.
5. Dip the filter into the water so one edge of the filter touches the water and use the clothespin to clip it to the side of the container to hold it upright. Getting the filter soaking wet all at once will wash away the color.
6. Watch the black color stretch out and separate into several colors as the dyes move at different rates with the water.

What to Talk About

1. Ask:
   - What happened to the lines of marker as the water moved up the paper filter?
   - How many colors can you see now?
   - Where did those colors come from? I thought we just used a black marker!? (Colors can be split.)

Books to Read

All the Colors We Are by Katie Kissinger
The Colors of Us by Karen Katz
Planting a Rainbow by Lois Ehlert
Rainbow Joe and Me by Maria Diaz Strom
Tell Me a Season by Mary McKenna Siddals

Follow-Up Activities

- Comment if a child is making new colors by mixing at the easel.

- Make "color tubes" by taping the acetate to the end of cardboard tubes. Look through them to see the world in different colors.
- At the Science Table, use watercolors to mix colors.
- Hang a prism in a sunny classroom window and look for rainbows.
- Outside on a bright sunny day you can see the colors that sunlight makes shining through a sheet of colored acetate onto a sheet of white paper. Then let it shine through colorless acetate. Ask, "What color did each of the acetate squares make when the sun shone through them?"
- Also outside, let the sun shine through a colorless prism, turning it until it creates a rainbow of light on the sheet of paper, as it separates the sunlight into many colors. Ask, "What color is the prism? What color(s) did the prism make?" (The prism separates the white light into many colors.)

Bringing Science Home!
A Note Home to Families About Mixing and Separating Colors

Dear Families,

Have you ever argued with a friend about whether a crayon is blue or green? An important observation the children made today was that colors can mix together to make new ones, even if we don't know what that color's name might be. Separating colors was as easy as mixing them because we were overlapping pieces of colored plastic and sliding them apart. Overlapping all the colors made a color so dark we couldn't see through it. It was as dark as the black marker we used to draw on a coffee filter. When we got the filter paper wet, imagine our surprise when we saw the black color began to separate into other colors!

Our Sense of Smell

Exploring Our Sense of Smell

Talk about when you notice smells. Talk about how the air smells inside and outside, during fall, winter, spring, and summer, on dry days and rainy days, and so on. Wonder aloud about how far away your nose can smell something.

Practice Sniffing

Materials
mirrors

What to Do
1. Have each child look in a mirror and practice sniffing.

What to Talk About
1. Ask:
   - How do we smell scents?
   - When do you notice a smell?
   - What is the sense of smell good for?

OBJECTIVE
To experience using our sense of smell and notice its limitations

SCIENCE TABLE
Put something new to smell each day, such as a lemon half, banana peel, or any fresh herbs from the garden or grocery store on the Science Table. (Put small or powdered materials in small containers covered with thin fabric.) Keep them out for a few weeks, or as long as you are exploring this experience with the children.

Each science experience has several activities, which, if done in sequence, build on each other. Doing everything from "To Get Ready" to "Follow-Up Activities" will give children repeated opportunities to understand concepts. The individual activities can be used separately, and children often want to repeat their favorite activities.

Animal Noses

Materials

pictures of good "animal smellers," such as a fly, mole, dog, pig, mosquito, or mouse

What to Do

1. Look at pictures of some of the best animal smellers (flies, pigs, dogs, moles, mosquitoes, and mice) and at any pictures you can find of interesting or unusual noses.

What to Talk About

1. Ask:
   - What do other animals like to sniff?
   - Why do noses come in different shapes?

Smell Guessing Games

Materials

opaque containers (small yogurt cups work well)
squares of flexible, opaque fabric
rubber bands
half of an onion
cinnamon stick
coffee beans
lemon balm
lemon-rose geranium
lemon grass or lemon verbena
half of a lemon

What to Do

1. Fill each container with one of the following sets:
   - Plants that have a similar smell, such as all lemon-like smelling plants, including lemon balm, lemon-rose geranium, lemon grass or lemon verbena, and half of a lemon.
   - Four objects that have very different smells, such as half of an onion, a cinnamon stick, half of a lemon, and coffee beans.

   Note: The lemon-scented herbs can be found at an herb nursery. They make wonderful additions to an herb garden. Lemon grass can be found in large grocery stores, or those that carry Asian foods.

2. Cover the containers with a flexible, opaque cloth. Hold in place with rubber bands.

   Note: Cover up any pictures on the containers because they are distracting to the children.

3. Encourage the children to guess what is in each set of containers before uncovering each container.

What to Talk About

1. The children will often name the smell by what food is commonly cooked or made with it, such as chicken for onion, and lemonade for lemon.

2. Ask:
   - Do we all sense the same smell?
   - Does something that smells good to me always smell good to other people? To other animals?
   - If something smells "bad" to us, should we eat it?

Books to Read

Dog Breath! The Horrible Trouble with Hally Tosis by Dav Pilkey

My Five Senses by Aliki

Smelling Things by Alan Fowler

Two Eyes, a Nose, and a Mouth by Roberta G. Intrater

Follow-Up Activities

- Plant an herb garden.
- Make a "Guess Whose Nose It Is" book using pictures of animals and people cut from magazines. Glue the pictures to stiff paper pages. On a blank page, mark the position of the nose in the picture. Cut a hole revealing just the nose when the blank page covers the picture page. These pages can be tied together or mounted in a 3-ring binder or folder so that the noses can be seen through the hole first, then turn the page and find out to whom the nose belongs!
- Children can have fun smelling while they draw with a cinnamon stick on a small piece of black emery paper, a type of sandpaper.

Bringing Science Home!
A Note Home to Families About Using Our Sense of Smell

Dear Families,

Lemonade! (lemon) Cereal! (cinnamon) Chicken! (onion) Coffee! (coffee beans) These are some of the answers the children gave to the question their nose asked: What am I smelling? The children were invited to play a smell guessing game. Isn't it interesting that the children identified lemon, cinnamon, and onion by a food name and not the individual ingredient name? Coffee was by far the most easily identified smell.

Children each favored different smells. Many children preferred lemon but a few chose onion.

Wheels Are Tools

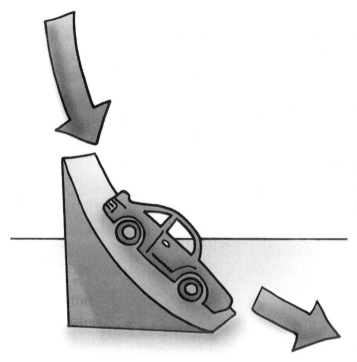

TO GET READY—

Exploring Wheels

Read a book about transportation (see list on page 201). Ask the children to talk about how wheels are used.

Moving a Variety of Shapes

Materials

variety of small, unbreakable objects (balls, small boxes, blocks, jars, lids, and so on)

What to Do

1. Look at a variety of classroom objects of varying shapes, such as small blocks, balls, and dolls.
2. Ask the children, "Which ones can you blow across the table?"

What to Talk About

1. Ask:
   - What shape moves (rolls) the easiest?
   - Where do you see this shape in the world?

⚲ Each science experience has several activities, which, if done in sequence, build on each other.
Doing everything from "To Get Ready" to "Follow-Up Activities" will give children repeated opportunities to understand concepts.
The individual activities can be used separately, and children often want to repeat their favorite activities.

ROLL?

SLIDE?

3. Ask the children to predict which objects will move by rolling, and which ones will move by sliding down the ramp.

4. To record the predictions, trace around the "Objects We Predict Will Roll" on one sheet of paper, and trace around the "Objects We Predict Will Slide" on another sheet of paper. Have them test their predictions by putting the objects, one at a time, at the top of the ramp and watching the result.

5. Record the results by tracing the objects again on another paper titled "These Objects Rolled" and "These Objects Slid." Compare the results with the predictions.

What to Talk About

1. Ask:
    - Did the object do what you predicted?
    - What shape did we trace onto the paper for the Objects That Rolled? (round)
    - What shape(s) did we trace onto the paper for the Objects That Slid? (square, rectangular, triangular)

Rollers and Sliders

Materials

variety of small, unbreakable objects (balls, small
    boxes, blocks, jars, lids, and so on)
lightweight board or cardboard
paper
markers

What to Do

1. This is an expanded version of the above activity.
2. Make a ramp by leaning a lightweight cardboard against a sturdy pile of blocks or bookshelf.

Prints of a Roller and a Slider

Materials

ball
square block (about the same size as the ball)
paper
paint

What to Do

1. Have the children make prints of a ball and of a square block by dipping the objects in paint and pressing them on to a large sheet of paper.

What to Talk About

1. Ask:
   - ⚲ Which object touches the paper the most: the round ball or the square block? (Balls, like wheels, touch just a little. Blocks, like boards, touch their whole bottom side. In the "Move a Heavy Load" activity below, dragging the bag of sand is harder than wheeling it in a wagon, because the wheels of the wagon barely touch the ground and, therefore, have much less friction with the ground.)

Move a Heavy Load

Materials

heavy bags of sand, such as 25- or 50-pound bags

What to Do

1. Tell the children that you have a group project—to move several bags of sand from across the playground (or down the sidewalk, down the hallway, or whatever fits your circumstance) to the sandbox (or another goal).
2. Encourage the children to try carrying, dragging, and pushing the heavy bags of sand.
3. After the children have tried to move the bags and have found it to be difficult, ask the children for their ideas on how to move the bags more easily.

What to Talk About

1. Ask:
   - ⚲ When you drag the bag of sand, where does it touch the ground?
   - ⚲ How big an area is touching the ground?

What Other Way Can We Move It?

Materials

heavy bags of sand, such as 25- or 50-pound bags
2 plywood boards about 2' x 3'
large-diameter dowels for rollers
2 10-foot lengths of rope
wagon

What to Do

1. Introduce children to the idea of using a board and rollers to move the heavy bags of sand.
2. Put large-diameter dowels under a sturdy board.
   Note: A free alternative to wooden dowels is to ask at flooring stores for the cardboard tubes that carpet or linoleum comes on.
3. To make the handle, drill a hole in the center of one end of the board. Loop a 10-foot length of rope through the hole and tie the ends together.
   Note: Warn the children to keep their fingers away from the board to prevent pinched fingers!
4. See if they come up with the idea of using a wagon by themselves. If not, suggest it.
5. Put the sandbags back for each new group of children to move.

What to Talk About

1. Ask:
   - ⚲ Why does using a wagon make the job easier?
   - ⚲ What touches the ground when you use rollers or a wagon?
   - ⚲ Does it touch more or less than the bag of sand being dragged?

Follow-Up Activity

⚲ Continue to talk about a variety of shapes. Ask the children, "Where do you see this shape in the world?"

Books to Read

Galimoto by Karen Lynn Williams

How Willy Got His Wheels by Deborahne Turner and Diana Mohler

Load 'Em Up Trucks (Mighty Wheels series) by Debora Pearson

What Is Round? by Rebecca Kai Dotlich

Wheels (Step into Reading) by Annie Cobb

Bringing Science Home!
A Note Home to Families About Wheels Are Tools

Dear Families,

Do you think children can move a 50-pound bag of sand? They did today by dragging it, by using tubes to roll it along, and then by wheeling it in a wagon. They worked hard! Guess which way was the easiest to move the sandbags?

In our study of wheels as tools, we noticed that wheels are round. We looked at objects of different shapes and made hypotheses about whether they would slide or roll down a ramp. As we tested them we put the objects into two groups, rollers or sliders. Guess what shape the rollers were?

Bubbles

OBJECTIVE
To experience making bubbles in a variety of ways with a variety of objects

SCIENCE TABLE

Materials

small, clear plastic bottles with tight-fitting lids

vegetable oil

water

bowl

food coloring

hot glue gun (adult only)

corn syrup

What to Do

1. Make two bubble toys.
2. For the first one, fill a small, clear plastic bottle almost to the top with vegetable oil, leaving space for about two tablespoons of colored water.
3. Add food coloring to a small bowl of water.
4. Add this colored water to the bottle to fill completely.
5. Seal the bottle by putting a small amount of hot glue inside the lid before tightly screwing on the lid.
6. Turn upside down to watch the water bubble move. Does the bubble move up or down? What shape is the bubble?
7. Make a second bottle by filling it with corn syrup, leaving a small space of air at the top.
8. Repeat step #5.
9. Turn the bottle over to watch the bubble of air move. Does the bubble move up or down? What shape is the bubble?
10. Keep the bubble toys on the Science Table for a few weeks, or as long as you are exploring this experience with the children.

Each science experience has several activities, which, if done in sequence, build on each other.
Doing everything from *To Get Ready* to *Follow-Up Activities* will give children repeated opportunities to understand concepts.
The individual activities can, of course, be used separately, and children often want to repeat their favorite activities.

TO GET READY—
Exploring Bubbles

Talk about feeling the air as the breeze moves, breathing in air, and puffing up your cheeks with air. Blow up balloons with air. Use shape names such as circle, square, sphere, and cube when referring to classroom objects.

Feel Air

Materials

straws

What to Do

1. Give each child a straw.
2. Blow through your straw onto your hand, and encourage the children to blow through their straws and feel the air coming through the straw.

What to Talk About

1. Be sure to remind the children to blow on to their hands, and not into their friends' faces.
2. Ask:
   - What do you feel?

Blow Air Into Water to Make Bubbles

Materials

small cups
straws

What to Do

1. Give each child a straw and a small cup that is half full of water.

What to Talk About

1. Ask:
   - What can you do with the cup of water and the straw? (They may need some

urging to feel comfortable blowing bubbles in the water because it is unacceptable to do at other times.)

2. Say, "I'm taking a breath, pulling air into my body, and now I'm going to let it out through the straw. The air went through the straw AND through the water."
3. Ask:
   - What did the air look like when it went through the water?
   - What shapes are the bubbles?
   - What are the bubbles made of?

What Is the Shape of a Bubble?

Materials

small clear plastic bottle
large clear container
water
a ball
a cube block (about the same size as the ball)

What to Do

1. Hold up a small clear bottle.
2. Ask, "What is filling the bottle?" (Air.)
3. Fill a large clear container part way with water.
4. Put the small container entirely into the water, open end first.
5. Slowly turn it right side up so the air bubbles escape. Repeat more than once.
6. Put a ball and a square block of approximately the same size where the children can see them easily.
7. Point to the ball and the block as examples of two kinds of shapes when you ask the children about the shape of the bubbles.

What to Talk About

1. Ask:
   - What is coming out of the bottle?
   - What are the bubbles made of? (Most

things that look empty are full of air. We saw air as it left the bottle and came up through the water.)

- What shapes are the bubbles? (They came out in round shapes called spheres. Many children may be uncertain about shape names. They may probably use the two-dimensional names—square and circle—to describe the cube-shaped block and the sphere-shaped ball. Ask them to point to the shape that is like the bubble shape.)

Can You Make a Square Bubble?

Materials
large, fuzzy pipe cleaners
bubble solution
shallow dishes
newspapers
towels

What to Do
1. Make a bubble wand out of long pipe cleaners, using extra fuzzy pipe cleaners or two regular ones twisted together.
2. Twist one end into a loop and bend the loop into a square shape, leaving the other end for a handle.
3. Spread newspaper or towels over the surface.
4. Pour bubble solution into a shallow dish.
5. Make bubbles by dipping the square bubble wand into the solution and blowing through the opening.
   Note: Use a portable fan (with a very fine mesh covering to keep small fingers safe) to provide the blowing power for younger children who can't yet coordinate sustained blowing. Window-unit air conditioners also work well, just make sure to cover the floor in front of it with newspapers or towels!

What to Talk About
1. Before blowing bubbles, say, "We're going to use this to blow bubbles. What shape bubble do you think this bubble wand will make?" (Refer to the ball and block. Resist the urge to make your own prediction.)
2. Ask:
   - What shapes are the bubbles?
   - What is inside the bubbles? (Very few preschoolers can describe the bubbles as being full of air. Ask this question just to get them thinking.)

Books to Read
Cubes, Cones, Cylinders, and Spheres by Tana Hoban
Is It Rough? Is It Smooth? Is It Shiny? by Tana Hoban
The Nature and Science of Bubbles by Jane Burton and Kim Taylor (for teachers)
Pop! : A Book About Bubbles by Kimberly Brubaker Bradley

Follow-Up Activity
- Once is never enough! Blow bubbles outside, vary the color of the bubble solution by adding food coloring, and vary the size of the bubbles by using a variety of bubble wands.

Bringing Science Home!
A Note Home to Families About Bubbles

Dear Families,

Bubbles in water and bubbles in air—children love to make, watch, and pop bubbles. We have been comparing the shape of the bubbles they made with the shape of a ball and the shape of a block. We have also been exploring whether it is possible to make a square bubble. Ask your child what he or she thinks.

To make a bubble toy, use a small, clear, plastic bottle that will not leak. Fill it with vegetable oil, leaving space for two tablespoons of colored water. Tightly screw the lid and seal with duct tape. To move the bubble of water, turn the bottle over. Does the bubble move up or down? Frequently check the seal of this bottle.

Recycling Paper to Use Again

OBJECTIVE
To introduce the idea of recycling finite resources by recycling newspaper into a new kind of paper or papier-mâché modeling dough

SCIENCE TABLE
Put objects made from recycled plastic or paper on the Science Table. Keep them out for a few weeks, or as long as you are exploring this experience with the children.

TO GET READY—

1. The week or day before, lead a discussion about reusing and recycling while doing these activities. Ask:
   - Does anyone recycle plastic or glass bottles, newspapers, or metal cans from their home?
   - What happens to the things that are recycled?
2. Read one of the suggested books (see page 212).

Feel Many Kinds of Paper

Materials
variety of papers

Each science experience has several activities, which, if done in sequence, build on each other. Doing everything from "To Get Ready" to "Follow-Up Activities" will give children repeated opportunities to understand concepts. The individual activities can be used separately, and children often want to repeat their favorite activities.

What to Do

1. With the children, examine paper made from a variety of materials such as brown paper bags, white computer paper, wrapping paper, and specialty papers, such as rice paper.

What to Talk About

1. Ask:
   - ? How are the papers the same, how are they different?
   - ? What are they made from?

What Does It Mean to Re-Use Something?

Materials
empty plastic container, such as a soda bottle

What to Do

1. Show the children an empty, plastic container, such as a soda bottle.
2. Ask them what else it could be used for now that the soda is gone.

What to Talk About

1. Ask:
   - ? Now that I'm finished with it, should I just throw it on the floor? (We can re-use many things, including bottles, clothes, and newspaper.)
2. Say, "I re-use newspaper to protect my table when I paint or to put wet boots on in the winter. What do you re-use?"

What Does It Mean to Recycle Something?

Materials
objects made from recycled material (examples below)

What to Do

1. Pass around an object made from a recycled material.
2. Some plastic buckets, polypropylene (fleece) fabric, rag rugs, and paper are labeled as being made from post-consumer recycled material. This means that it was made from material that was used by consumers (that's us!).

What to Talk About

1. When used bottles are melted together, the melted plastic is recycled into another shape. It can be spun into thread to make fabric or shaped into another kind of bottle. Say, "Can you believe that this fleece vest is made of melted plastic soda bottles?"
2. The same material can be shaped into a different object.
3. When a lot of used paper is mixed together with water, it can be recycled, or made into new paper.

Prepare for Recycling Paper

Materials

newspaper
blender
bowl, bucket, or dishpan
water
nylon stocking, pantyhose leg, or screen sieve
resealable plastic bag or container

What to Do

1. Up to a week ahead, for a group of 12 children tear up two full sheets (double page) of newspaper into squares, 2" wide or less, and soak them in a bowl of water for 1 to 8 hours.
2. In a blender set at high speed, puree ½ cup of presoaked newspaper at a time with 2 cups of water. The water is necessary to keep the blender blade from jamming and burning out the motor.
3. Pour the newspaper pulp into an old nylon stocking to strain out enough water to make the paper pulp the consistency of a wet playdough, or as one child noted, tuna fish salad. A screen sieve can also be used to strain out the extra water.
4. Transfer the strained pulp to a resealable plastic bag or container.

5. Repeat the process until all the newspaper is pureed.
6. Store the pulp in the refrigerator until the day you use it.

Change the Shape of Newspaper

Materials

newspapers
blender
water

What to Do

1. Tell your class that you have learned how to recycle newspaper.
2. Let the children help tear up a small amount of newspaper and puree it in a blender with water to show how it changes from a flat sheet with type printed on it to a uniformly gray pulp.
   Note: Some children may be sensitive to the sound of the blender. To help them tolerate it, encourage the children to mimic the noise and suggest that they cover their ears or leave the room before starting the blender.

What to Talk About

1. Say, "Now that we have put all the little pieces of newspaper into the water, I'm going to turn on the blender. It's going to make a noise like this: "BRRrrrr.""
2. Ask:
   - What do you think will happen to the newspaper?
   - Did the blender change the newspaper?

Recycled Paper, Step 1

Materials

paper pulp from activity on page 209

metal window screen

rectangular tub

sponge

white glue

towels or lots of extra newspapers to soak up the
    water

What to Do

1. After a demonstration of the following
   process, most four-year-olds can manage
   most of it themselves.
2. Cover the table with a waterproof
   tablecloth and a stack of newspapers or old
   towels to absorb the excess water.
3. Pour the blended paper pulp from the
   blender into a rectangular tub,
   approximately 12" x 18".
4. Add water to a depth of about four inches.
   Add a handful or two of previously blended
   pulp to the mixture and stir.

5. Slide a 9" x 12" square of metal window
   screen down into the mixture, under the
   suspended pulp and lift slowly.
   Note: Cover all sharp ends of the screen
   with duct tape.
6. The children may need help with the next
   part. Keeping the screen level so the water
   drips out but the pulp mostly stays on the
   screen, slowly lift up the screen.

What to Talk About

1. Ask:
   - What is happening to the water?
   - What is happening to the paper pulp?

Recycled Paper, Step 2

Materials

paper pulp on window screen from previous
    activity

sponge

towels or lots of extra newspapers to soak up the
    water

What to Do

1. When the water stops dripping from the
   window screen, put the screen down on a
   section of newspaper, cover with another
   section, and, using your hands like a
   squeegee, press out more water.
2. The harder you press, the more cohesive
   your new piece of paper will be. Keep a
   large sponge handy to soak up the water.
3. Next, turn the entire stack of newspaper
   over, open to the screen, and lift the screen
   up from the now compressed paper pulp.
4. When it dries, this recycled paper can be
   peeled from the newspaper.

What to Talk About

1. Say, "We made a new paper out of newspapers. Is the paper ready to write on or cut into shapes now? What has to happen before we can use this recycled paper? (It must dry.) When do you think it will be dry?" (It will take one or two days to dry.)

Making Papier-Mâché From Newspapers

Materials

newspapers
bowl
blender
screen sieve or nylon stocking
rectangular tub
sponge
white school glue
towels or lots of extra newspapers to soak
    up the water

What to Do

1. Make a playdough-like paper pulp following the process described in the "Prepare for Recycling Paper" on page 209. To make a drier dough, drain out much of the water by putting the pulp in an old nylon stocking and squeezing it.

2. Add about ½ cup white school glue to 4 cups of fairly dry pulp and mix well. It works best if you use your hands. Some children will love to help!

3. This pulp can be shaped into small bowls or used to cover a framework to make a larger object. Young children enjoy making "tortillas" and "pancakes." Place a ball on a craft stick and cover it with this papier-mâché to create a great puppet head. Then, paint it when it's dry. Make a cone shape and stick a small medicine bottle or film canister inside to create a volcano.
Note: A pad of newspaper underneath the work surface makes moving the artwork, and cleaning up, easier.

What to Talk About

1. Ask:
    🔑 Do you like the way the recycled paper dough feels?
    We made a kind of playdough out of newspapers. We're using them again in a new way.

The Resources of the Earth Are Precious

Materials
photograph of the Earth

What to Do
1. Look at a photograph of the Earth.

What to Talk About
1. Ask:
   - Where in this picture do the plants used in making paper grow?
2. Show children the parts of the Earth that are water and the parts that are land. With older children, continue the discussion by asking what would happen if all the paper-making trees were used up.
3. Ask:
   - How long does it take a tree to grow?
   - Do you think we could use old paper over again?

Books to Read
Crushed, Smashed, and Mashed by Joyce Slayton Mitchell

Each Living Thing by Joanne Ryder

The Earth Is Good: A Chant in Praise of Nature by Michael DeMunn

Here Comes the Recycling Truck! by Meyer Seltzer

Recycle That! by Fay Robinson

Recycle: A Handbook for Kids by Gail Gibbons

This Is Our Earth by Laura Lee Benson

You're Aboard Spaceship Earth by Patricia Lauber

Website to Visit
See the Science Museum of Minnesota's version of recycled paper at www.sci.mus.mn.us.

Bringing Science Home!
A Note Home to Families About Recycling Paper

Dear Families,

Taking care of the Earth takes on new meaning when we become parents because somebody we love will be on this Earth when we have passed on. When talking to our children about taking care of the Earth, we know that positive encouragement is more likely to change our children's behavior than negative comments, such as "Don't litter!" or "Stop wasting water!" Two books that celebrate the Earth are This Is Our Earth *by Laura Lee Benson and* The Earth Is Good: A Chant in Praise of Nature *by Michael DeMunn.*

The words "repair, reuse, recycle" encourage us to make the best use of our possessions before we replace them. The children found out that they can turn old newspapers into something they can use for artwork. We soaked newspaper scraps, put them through the blender with some water, added some school glue, and mixed. It was sticky! Your child turned this wonderful paper dough into some interesting things that will be coming home soon, after they are dry.

As parents, we're aware that our example speaks much louder than our words. Your child may ask you what things your family reuses or recycles. You can talk about hand-me-down clothing and toys, the trash can made of recycled plastic bags, and you can show your child the words on the cereal boxes that tell how much recycled paper went into making it.

Rocket Ships Blasting Off

(Thanks to NASA for the rocket instructions. Note that the effervescing antacid tablet (Alka-Seltzer®) contains aspirin. Keep unopened packages in your pocket and pick up undissolved pieces immediately after blast off to prevent the children from eating any of it.)

OBJECTIVES
To experience what happens when one kind of solid is mixed with water, a liquid
To have fun pretending with rockets

SCIENCE TABLE
Materials

large cardboard box	recyclable containers
tape and glue	scissors
pillows	stick-on Velcro
notepads, pencils	forks and spoons
empty snack food bags, mirrored on the inside	

1. Help the children make a child-size spaceship (or two) out of a large cardboard box and make control panel instruments using all kinds of small recyclable containers.
2. Cut out portholes, attach cardboard rocket fins, and put pillows inside.
3. Use stick-on Velcro to hold down notepads, pencils, forks, and spoons.
4. Keep the spaceship out for a few weeks, or as long as you are exploring this experience with the children.
5. Cover the outside with the mirrored side of some snack food bags.

TO GET READY—
Exploring Rocket Ships

Materials
books about space or rocket ships (see suggestions on page 217)
Mylar (metallic plastic wrapping paper) or regular paper
film canister with an inward-fitting lid
tape
stickers and markers
scissors

1. Read one of the suggested books.
2. Talk about traveling into space in a rocket.
3. Help the children make a toy rocket ship.

♀ Each science experience has several activities, which, if done in sequence, build on each other.
Doing everything from "To Get Ready" to "Follow-Up Activities" will give children repeated opportunities to understand concepts.
The individual activities can be used separately, and children often want to repeat their favorite activities.

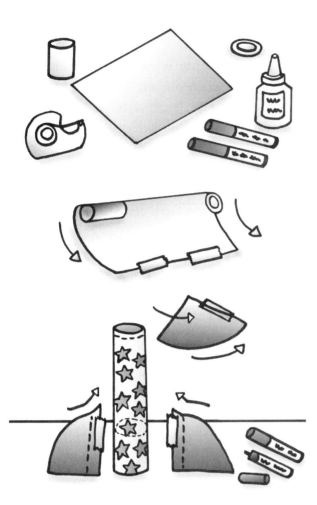

Note: For safety reasons, adults must be in control of the rocket launch. Therefore, it might be best to make only one rocket to launch, so it is clear that the children will not be making their own rocket blast off. The children can handle the materials, cut out the shapes, and help tape or glue some material to paper or make rocket pictures to take home.

4. Use Mylar (plastic wrapping paper) and a film canister that has an inward fitting lid, not the kind of lid that snaps down over the canister.

5. Wrap and tape a tube from a 4" x 8" piece of Mylar around the film canister to make the body of the rocket. The lid end of the film canister goes down (the rocket rests on it) and is exposed at the bottom.

   Note: Paper can be used instead of Mylar, although it falls apart more quickly.

6. Tape fins to the rocket if desired, and decorate with stickers or markers.

7. Cut out a small half-circle and roll it into a cone to make the pointy top.

8. Tape it to the rocket's upper end.

How Do Rockets Work?

Materials

pictures of rockets, spaceships, astronauts, and the Earth and Moon from space
toy rockets, spaceships, astronauts, and satellites

What to Do

1. Look at pictures of rockets blasting off and play with toy spaceships.

What to Talk About

1. Ask:
   - How do the rockets get up into the sky?
   - What pushes them there?
   - Why are the ends of the rockets a bright red color?
   - How hot are they?

The Power of Gas

Materials

bottle of club soda

What to Do

1. Shake a closed club soda bottle and open the lid slightly.

What to Talk About

1. Ask:
   - What is coming out? (Bubbles of gas.)
   - Do you remember when we erupted the pretend volcano and all the pretend lava bubbled out? (The gas made bubbles, like gas from the soda bottle. Our pretend volcano wasn't hot, but real volcanoes are hot. We put baking soda and vinegar together to erupt the pretend volcano. We are going to put two things together to make a pretend rocket blast off, just like we put two things together to make a volcano erupt.)

Fuel for the Pretend Rocket

Materials

Alka-Seltzer
water
clear glass

What to Do

1. Ask the children what they think will happen when you put the solid Alka-Seltzer tablet into the liquid water.
2. Put the tablet into a clear glass of water.
   Note: Because the Alka-Seltzer has aspirin in it, do not let the children handle it.

What to Talk About

1. Ask:
   "What do you see?" (Bubbles of gas.)

Blast Off!

Materials

rocket from activity on page 214
towels
Alka-Seltzer
water bottle

What to Do

1. Fold a towel in half to use as the launch pad.
2. Ask the children to pass around the Mylar rocket.
3. Remind them that it is a pretend rocket and will not get hot.
4. Ask a child to help you fill the rocket's fuel (film) canister ¼ full of water and show it to all the children.
   Note: For safety reasons, adults must be in control of the rocket launch.

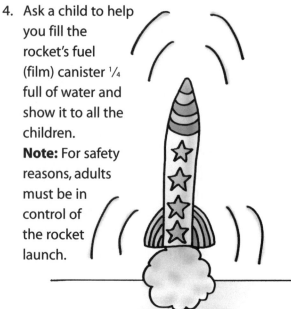

5. Put ¼ of an Alka-Seltzer tablet in the canister with the water. Immediately cap the canister and set the rocket upright on the floor to prepare for blast off (adult only). It usually takes about 15 to 25 seconds for the rocket to blast off. The rocket will rise about 5-15 feet.

What to Talk About

1. Before putting the Alka-Seltzer in the water, ask:
   - ֎ What do you think will happen when I put the solid Alka-Seltzer in the water?
2. Quick, snap the lid on! Stand back to give the rocket room to lift off!
   - ֎ What will it sound like when the rocket blasts off?

   We can put our fingers in our ears now, if we don't like loud sounds.
3. When rockets are sent into space, the space center has a countdown. They count backwards and hope that when they reach zero the rocket will blast off. Say, "Let's do a COUNT DOWN! 10, 9, 8, 7, 6, 5, 4, 3, 2, 1, 0, BLASTOFF!"

   Note: The countdown ending will rarely happen at the moment the rocket lifts off. Just do another, shorter countdown.
4. Ask:
   - ֎ What pushed the rocket up?

Books to Read

Blast Off!: A Space Counting Book by Norma Cole
Cutaway Space Vehicles by Jon Richards
Eyewitness: Space Exploration by Carole Stott
I Want to Be an Astronaut by Byron Barton
Space Exploration by Carole Stott
The Space Shuttle by Jacqueline Langille and
    Bobbie Kalman

Website to Visit

The National Aeronautics and Space Administration website includes a teacher's guide, *Rockets*, published in February 1996.
http://spaceplace.jpl.nasa.gov/rocket.htm

Follow-Up Activities

- ֎ Prepare a snack for space! Cheese sticks, applesauce in small containers, and box juices are similar to the packaging of meals in space. Use stick-on Velcro to fasten down the packages!
- ֎ Make space helmets from paper grocery bags and use adult-sized gloves for astronaut dress-up. Have the children try doing work in space while wearing the gloves. It's not easy!

Bringing Science Home!
A Note Home to Families About Rocket Ships Blasting Off

Dear Families,

We have been exploring many questions about rocket ships, including:

- *How do the rockets get up into the sky?*
- *What pushes them there?*
- *Why are the ends of the rockets a bright red color?*
- *How hot are they?*

The National Aeronautics and Space Administration (NASA) website includes a rocket-building project in its teacher's guide, Rockets, published in February 1996. Look for it on the web at: spacelink.nasa.gov/Instructional.Materials/ NASA.Educational.Products/Rockets.

We made a rocket ship of our own. Our pretend rockets weren't hot at all. To make them blast off with a loud pop, the children put a little water and an adult put part of an Alka-Seltzer tablet into the water into the film canister at the base of our pretend rocket. The class chanted the countdown and the rocket did blast off!

We are having a lot of fun pretending with rockets. The non-fiction section of the library is a good place to find books with actual photographs of rockets and of people living and working in space. Maybe your child will go to space someday.

Making Solutions

OBJECTIVE

To introduce the concept of a solid dissolving in a liquid

SCIENCE TABLE

Materials

salt
hot water
shallow tray
dark construction paper
paintbrushes

What to Do

1. Make a solution with a high salt content. Start with very hot water and add as much salt as can be dissolved in the water, then add two more tablespoons.
2. Pour the solution into a shallow tray.
3. The children can use paintbrushes to pick up some salt water with each dip and dab or splash it on dark construction paper.
4. Watch the salt crystals appear as the water evaporates.
5. Put the salt crystals on the Science Table and keep them out for a few weeks, or as long as you are exploring this experience with the children.

What to Talk About

1. Ask:
♀ What will happen when the water dries up (evaporates)?

TO GET READY—

Exploring Solutions

Talk about evaporation in everyday situations. If it rains, say, "There was a big puddle on the blacktop yesterday and now it's smaller. Why is that? Where did the rest of the water go?"

Identifying Plain Water

Materials

plastic spoons
water in a pitcher or water bottle

What to Do

1. Show the children a pitcher with water in it.
2. Taste it first and then let the children taste the water by pouring a little into their plastic spoon.

♀ Each science experience has several activities, which, if done in sequence, build on each other.
Doing everything from "To Get Ready" to "Follow-Up Activities" will give children repeated opportunities to understand concepts.
The individual activities can be used separately, and children often want to repeat their favorite activities.

What to Talk About

1. Ask:
   - What do you think is in the pitcher?
   - Is it just plain water?
   - Is it wet?
   - Is it a liquid, a solid, or a gas?

Identify the Solids

Materials
sand
sugar
bowls

What to Do

1. Put a cup of sand in one bowl and a cup of sugar in another bowl.
2. Show the children the two solids in two bowls, one containing sugar and one containing sand.
3. After some discussion about what they are, have willing children taste a pinch of the solids to help identify them.

What to Talk About

1. Ask:
   - Are they wet or dry?
   - What do you think they are?
   - How can we find out?
2. If we know these substances are safe to eat, we can taste them to help us decide what they are. I know that these two solids are safe to taste. Always ask a grown-up before you taste something unknown.

3. Use a serving spoon to put small amounts of sugar on the children's spoons. Ask, "Was it what you thought it was?"
4. Then give them just a few grains of sand to taste. The children will think it strange that you are suggesting they taste the sand. Remind them that they have probably tasted sand before, perhaps accidentally, from the sandbox or at the beach. Ask, "Does the sand taste like the sugar?"
5. Ask:
   - Are they solids, liquids, or gases?
   - What do you think will happen when we mix each of these substances with water?
   - What is your hypothesis?

Mix the Liquid and the Solids

Materials
clear plastic cups or plastic jars
    with tight-fitting lids
plastic spoons
sugar
sand
paper
markers, crayons
towels

What to Do

1. Preschoolers enjoy having their own clear plastic cup and a spoon for stirring the water and sugar together.

2. Help the children put about ¹⁄₂ cup of water and 1 heaping teaspoon of sugar into their cups. Keep a towel nearby to wipe up spills. **Note:** If spills are a problem, put the water in each of two plastic jars. Add 1 heaping teaspoon of sugar to one jar, and 1 heaping teaspoon of sand to the other jar. Be sure to show the children that it is important to put the lids on tightly.

3. Have the children stir their cups (or shake both jars) for a few minutes. Encourage them to shake the containers while they dance to a song to keep it interesting. If using jars, be sure each child has a turn, passing the jars from one child to the next after one verse.

4. Sing (to the tune of the "Caribbean Calypso" song or to a tune of your own invention):

   *Stir your cup (or shake your jar) to the
       calypso beat,*
   Give a little wiggle and move your feet,
   Stir your cup to the calypso beat,
   Give a little wiggle and find your seat.

   *(Or if using the jars)…and pass it to your
   neighbor.*

   ♀ This adaptation was made from the Caribbean Calypso song on *Multicultural Rhythm Stick Fun* from Kim 9028 Multicultural Rhythm Stick Fun, Kimbo International, Long Branch, NJ.

What to Talk About

1. Ask:
   ♀ What do you think will happen when we put the dry solid into the wet liquid?
   ♀ Who wants sugar in their cup and who wants sand? Almost all children will

choose sugar; therefore, make a cup with sand for yourself. Say, "I think I will put sand into my cup."
   ♀ What do you think will happen when we mix these two substances together, the wet and the dry, the liquid and the solid?
   ♀ What is your hypothesis?

2. If you can, record the children's hypotheses with drawings or words.

Comparing the Results

Materials

cups or jars from previous activity

What to Do

1. Stop shaking or stirring and look into the cups.

2. Compare the cups or jar containing the sugar with those containing the sand.

What to Talk About

1. Ask:
   ♀ What do you see?
   ♀ What is happening?
   ♀ Where is the sugar?
   ♀ Where is the sand?
   ♀ Did the sugar fall out?
   ♀ How can we find out if it is still in the water?

Taste the Water to Find the Sugar

Materials

cups or jars from previous activity
plastic spoons
slice of lemon for each child

What to Do

1. When the sugar crystals are completely dissolved, taste the liquid again by having the children sip from their cups or by pouring a small amount from the jar into the children's spoons.
2. Children with their own cups may enjoy making lemonade by adding a slice of lemon to their sugar solution.

What to Talk About

1. Ask:
   - What did you taste?
   - Is the sugar still in the water? (The sugar is all mixed into the water.) The sugar is dissolved in the water to make a solution. A solution is a special kind of mixture that is evenly mixed (homogenous).
   - Is the sand dissolved?
   - Did it make a solution with the water?
   - Is this what you thought might happen?

2. Refer to their recorded hypotheses.
3. Ask:
   - What if sand were made of sugar?
   - What would the sandbox be like?
   - What would the beach be like?

Follow-Up Activities

- Divide the sugar solution between two jars. Open one of the two jars but put the lid on the other one. Note the change during the week in the open jar as water evaporates. Each day check to see if any sugar crystals can be seen in the open jar. If so, point this out to the children. The water leaves the jar as tiny particles, too tiny to see.
- Make lemonade again!

Bringing Science Home!
A Note Home to Families About Making Solutions

Dear Families,

What happens when we mix two things together? Something dry, such as sugar, and something wet, such as water? The children were very excited as we discussed this question, and they eagerly carried out the procedure.

We put two teaspoons of sugar into about half a cup of water and shook it! (We were careful to close the lid tightly.) Everybody got to shake the jar and everybody got to say what they thought happened. "It disappeared!" was the most common conclusion. We found that "disappeared" is not the same as "went away" because when we tasted the now clear water, it tasted sweet. Why was that? The water dissolved the sugar and together they made a sugar solution.

The sand that the class mixed with water and shook never disappeared. It did not dissolve and make a solution with the water. It's a good thing there isn't sugar in the sandbox!

Your children may enjoy making a special solution at home by stirring two teaspoons of sugar into half a cup of water and adding flavor such as a slice of lemon.

Measuring Hands

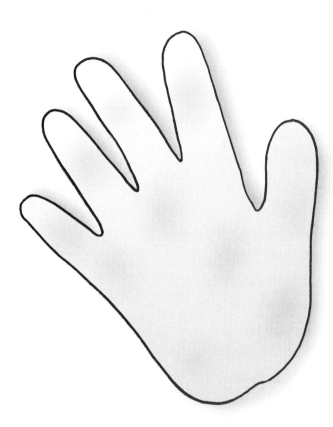

Exploring Measuring

Talk with the children about size, using words such as *large, small, tiny, wide, narrow, tall, short,* and *medium.* Include the idea that each size is good for something; bigger is not necessarily better. Sometimes short children are reluctant to discuss height as many people associate taller height with being grown up and, therefore, more competent.

Make a Set of Measuring Hands

Materials

construction paper
pencils
scissors
clear contact paper (or access to lamination)
tape
ribbon

What to Do

1. Make a length-measuring tool for classroom use. Instead of inches or centimeters, this measuring tool uses hands.
2. Use a pencil to trace around each child's hand onto construction paper, or use paint handprints that are dry.
   Note: The paper hands will last longer if the fingers are not spread out wide.

OBJECTIVE
To introduce measuring, a tool of scientists, and use our hands as a unit of measure

SCIENCE TABLE
Put the following items on the Science Table. Keep them out for a few weeks, or as long as you are exploring this experience with the children.
- *The measuring hands ribbon (see directions at right)*
- *Other measuring tools, such as a tape measure or ruler*

Each science experience has several activities, which, if done in sequence, build on each other.
Doing everything from "To Get Ready" to "Follow-Up Activities" will give children repeated opportunities to understand concepts.
The individual activities can be used separately, and children often want to repeat their favorite activities.

3. Trace two hands for each child so one hand can be labeled with the child's name to use for the next activity (or to take home), and the other decorated or left blank to use in the Measuring Hands Set.

4. After the children have left, tape each hand to a long piece of ribbon, with the fingertips just touching the bottom of the previous palm so the hands lie in a long continuous line.

5. Laminate the hands or use clear contact paper to cover the entire hand measure, making a wide "ribbon" of hands.

2. When everyone's hands are traced, we can tape them end-to-end and use them to measure things.

Measure With a Hand

Materials
construction paper
pencils
scissors
clear contact paper (or access to lamination)
markers, crayons

What to Do
1. Use a pencil to trace around each child's hand onto construction paper, or use one of the handprints from the previous activity. **Note:** The paper hands will last longer if the fingers are not spread out wide and are laminated or covered in clear contact paper.

2. Each child decorates one of his or her hands and compares its length to objects in the classroom.

What to Talk About
1. Ask:
   - ᕃ Is your hand as long as a unit block?
   - ᕃ Is your hand longer than a baby's hand?
   - ᕃ How many hands do you think it would take to be as long as the fire truck?

What to Talk About
1. Ask:
   - ᕃ How long is your hand?
     My hand is THIS long.
   - ᕃ How long is the sink/table/puzzle?
   - ᕃ How tall is the swing set /slide/ monkey bars on the playground?
   - ᕃ How many hands tall is it?

Measure With Many Hands

Materials
measuring hands ribbon from previous activity
pencils
scissors
clear contact paper (or access to lamination)
tape or ribbon

What to Do
1. Once the hand measure is laminated or covered in clear contact paper, it can be used for measuring bodies, tables, distance to the bathroom, and so on.
2. If size is a sensitive issue or competition is too great for measuring body size, try comparing the length of forearms or the distance around children's heads, as those measurements are almost always very similar.
3. Measure the wall up to the estimated height of a former teacher, a favorite book character, or an animal, real or imagined.

What to Talk About
1. Ask:
   - What is your hat size?
   - How tall a doorway would we need to get Clifford, The Big Red Dog, into our school?
   - What can we tell someone with the length we just measured?
   - Why do scientists want to measure things? (Scientists measure things so they can talk about relative size with other scientists and compare the things they study to other things.)

Books to Read
How Tall, How Short, How Faraway by David A. Adler
Length by Henry Pluckrose
Measuring Penny by Loreen Leedy

Follow-Up Activities
- Show how many hands high one of the smaller dinosaurs would have stood and compare to how many hands high one of the larger ones would have stood. Measure any growing plants. Pole bean vines are especially fun to measure because they grow taller than the children, and they grow quickly.
- Older children may want to use standard measuring tools such as a ruler or tape measure.

Bringing Science Home!
A Note Home to Families About Measuring Hands

Dear Families,

How big is it? How tall, how wide, or how long are questions that we ask about the lengths of things. Scientists measure things so they can compare them with other things, or so they can tell another scientist the length of the measurement. So do children! We decided we could use our hands to measure lengths. Hands are not standard units like meters or inches. For children, measuring with the length of an actual object (such as a hand) makes the measured length easier to visualize. When all the children's hands are lined up, the class is able to measure large lengths. How many hands high do you think a baby Tyrannosaurus Rex dinosaur would be?

Writing Additional Lessons

The experiences in this book usually began with a gift from children—the joy of watching them make discoveries as they played. I saw that I could lead the children towards discovery of a particular science concept by providing the necessary materials while they played. So although the science lessons in this book begin with a title, they really began with an activity, or sometimes an object a child brought to show me. Then they evolved with a question, "How can I set up additional activities that flow, with little adult involvement, to the children's discovery and exploration of the science concept?" Or in the case of objects such as an acorn or a rock, "How can I set up additional activities that flow, with little adult involvement, to the children's discovery of the history or future of the object?"

What science concepts and activities are missing from this book? What experiences have you witnessed in your classrooms that are not represented in any of the activities? These are the lessons that you write. Think of the lesson plan as a recipe for discovery. The more descriptive you are, the more valuable it will be next year when you want to use it again and the more valuable it will be to the teacher who says, "What were you doing in your classroom? Can we do it too?"

What to Do

Which activity or object do you want to explore? If the children have a new-found enjoyment of water play on the first warm day that you were able to bring out the water table, if they were busy discovering that water behaves differently than the dry materials that filled the table for the last several months, the children might say, "Water is wet!" And you might respond, "Yes, it is a liquid."

Then think about an activity that would help children discover the qualities of "wetness" or that examines substances that are liquid. Describe the activity and how you can make it extensive and accessible. How can you set it up in a way that maximizes the children's safe involvement from start to finish? How can you minimize adult control? You might write, "Play with water in a water table. Have the children help set up the table by carrying water to the table in a variety of containers, and clean up after the activity with cloth towels."

To continue the lesson, describe another activity that expands on or builds on the first one. Write it as a "recipe" for another teacher. A recipe in progress, because every time you use the activity plan, the children will teach you new ways of using the material. For the exploration of water-as-a-liquid example, you might write, "Blow into small cups of water with straws, make an herbal tea, or make and melt ice."

There are many reasons why we limit children's direct exploration. For safety reasons some activities, though instructive, are off limits. The amount of time you have may limit the amount of discovery. Our reluctance to get messy, knowing in advance how much work is required afterward to clean the classroom (and the children) can stop us from going as far with an activity as the children need to fully experience the material. Find ways around these obstacles. You may have to tell families repeatedly that the children are going to get messy and should come to school dressed to do so. Look for alternatives, options, and other routes to learning, such as doing the experience outside where spilled water is not a problem, or doing just part of it when time is an issue.

Listing Materials

When listing materials, list everything, especially the obvious, such as water. When you grab a lesson plan to find out if you can do it next month, next week, or tomorrow, it is very important to have everything within reach. Having the children sit and wait is not productive to making scientific or any other kind of discoveries. Words cannot substitute for doing, seeing, or feeling.

What to Talk About

For the "What to Talk About" sections, write questions that will encourage children to describe their experiences.

- What will happen if…?
- Why do you think it does…?
- How much water do you think we need to fill the table?
- How can we get it to the table?
- What do you see/hear/feel/taste/smell?
- How does this compare to that?

Encourage the children to make hypotheses about what they think will happen, and try to test them.

Read nonfiction children's books on the topic. Children's librarians love to help develop an idea with books on the subject and related children's literature. Write down the information from the books that you think will be a good fit for preschoolers and information that was new to you to ensure that you have the big picture, or at least a slightly bigger picture than the one you hope to share with the children.

Write a note reminding yourself NOT to answer the questions unless it's a direct request for information. Encourage children to find out information for themselves. If it is within their abilities, let them do the work to find out. Rework your activity plan to make it happen. But if they ask how a magnet is made, or what is the name of an insect, or something they cannot discover by themselves, look it up with them in a book or tell them the information that you know.

Selecting Books

For the "Books to Read" section, list books, tapes, and compact discs. Children's literature for threes, fours, and fives often has science concepts woven into the story or illustrations. Ask your librarian for help. Try to find one nonfiction book for each lesson that can be useful to the adults if not the children. Is there a song on an audiotape or compact disc that relates to your lesson? Fingerplays are also a great way of expanding the lesson.

In addition, look at the books of poems on specific subjects such as nature. Collections of poems are often beautifully illustrated so a pre-reader will enjoy leafing through them. Many poems are short enough for preschoolers and fingerplays can be invented around them.

Writing a Title

Now that you know what you want to do with the children, what is a good name for describing the experience to adults?

What Are the Objectives?

Write down what you want the children to explore. Two general objectives are:

- To provide activities that will lead to asking questions about and thinking about (fill in the blank).
- To focus the children's attention on (fill in the blank) that we see happening in our world.

To Get Ready

Once you know what science lesson the class will be doing, this part is easier to write. What groundwork is necessary to introduce some of the language or some of the materials to the classroom? For our example, you might want to make a conscious effort to use the word liquid when you are drinking at snack time. If you want the children to think about the why of something, it's best to let them fully explore the material, to become very familiar with its nature before you ask them to pause and reflect.

Follow-Up Activities

Describe another activity (or activities) that can be done in a different setting, with slightly different materials, or with a different size group. List activities that repeat the experience in a new way, or expand upon it. This might be where you write what you want to do someday when you have the money to buy special materials. Using the water example, you could take the lesson in a new direction, exploring how animals live in water by setting up a fish and snail tank.

Science Table

Your "table" might be a shelf or a basket. Any place is fine to hold objects for a few weeks to allow further exploration as the children desire. Make it something that every child can handle safely and without it breaking. Two weeks is the longest any one object should remain on the Science Table unless it is a tool for exploring other objects, such as a magnifying glass. You might want to have a separate "Scientists' Tools" area.

Bringing Science Home

In this section, explain to the children's parents about how the children can "do" science at school. Invite them to come by and look at the Science Table, to ask their children questions, or to read

their children a suggested book. Give parents the knowledge to be part of the process. Tell them what the children did and what some of the children said, and give a little more information than you gave the children. Although this is a generic note by necessity, it is the pebble that you drop to make ever-widening circles. It is the first step to empowering the children and their parents to be comfortable working scientifically—to ask questions and seek to answer them.

The Layout of the Lesson Plan

Reassemble your lesson plan in this order and you will be ready to go.

TITLE
OBJECTIVE(S)
SCIENCE TABLE
TO GET READY
THE ACTIVITIES
   ♀   Title
   ♀   Materials
   ♀   What to Do
   ♀   What to Talk About
BOOKS TO READ
FOLLOW-UP ACTIVITIES
BRINGING SCIENCE HOME!

APPENDIX

Resources

Complete Book List

Out-of-Print Book List

Resources

Magazines

Ladybug, The magazine for young children. A rich source of seasonal stories and poems, many of which include science concepts, as well as occasional science activities. The youngest preschoolers will prefer *Babybug.*
1-800-827-0227
www.ladybugmag.com

Science & Children
National Science Teachers Association
1840 Wilson Blvd.
Arlington, VA 22201-3000
1-800-722-6782
www.nsta.org

Your Big Backyard, a magazine for children from the National Wildlife Federation
1-800-611-1599
www.nwf.org.ybby

Places to Buy Materials

If possible, don't buy materials—look in your neighbors' recycling tubs on trash day. Ask the children's families to save containers for you.

Many items can be purchased at school supply stores, craft stores, and party stores.

General Catalogues:

For all sorts of science equipment including live animals:
Carolina Biological Supply Company
(request the full catalogue, not just K-3)
1-800-334-5551
www.carolina.com

Delta Education
1-800-442-5444
www.delta-ed.com

Frey Scientific
1-800-225-FREY
www.freybg.com

The Astronomical Society of the Pacific
1-800-335-2624
www.aspsky.org

Specific Items:

Beeswax:
Bee Supply Catalog
The A.I. Root Company
1-800-289-7668

Fossils:
Visit a rock and mineral show to find out about local fossil dealers like Tom Taaffe of KBT Minerals in the Washington, D.C. area. Check websites such as the one for Rockhounds Information Page at www.rahul.net/infordyn/rockhounds.htm

Photo of the Earth:
Sky and Telescope Magazine catalogue
1-800-253-0245
www.skypub.com

Plants:
Thompson and Morgan, Ltd.
1-800-274-7333
www.thompson-morgan.com

Sandy Mush Herb Nursery
828-683-2014
www.brwm.org/sandymushherbs/mailing.ht

Fun Websites to Browse for Ideas and Information

The Academy of Natural Sciences
www.acnatsci.org

American Museum of Natural History
www.amnh.org

bugbios
www.bugbios.com

Eisenhower National Clearinghouse, see Focus, a magazine that helps educators incorporate children's literature into math and science curricula.
www.enc.org/focus/lit

The Franklin Institute in Philadelphia, Pennsylvania
www.fi.edu

Miami Museum of Science
www.miamisci.org

The Museum of Science, Art and Human Perception in San Francisco
www.exploratorium.edu

Museum of Science, Boston
www.mos.org

National Aeronautics and Space Administration, NASA
www.spacelink.nasa.gov/

National Science Foundation, see education community links for sites recommended for and by educators
www.nsf.gov

Oregon Museum of Science and Industry
www.omsi.edu

Science Learning Network
www.sln.org

Science Museum of Minnesota
www.sci.mus.mn.us

The Smithsonian
www.si.edu

The Virtual Insectary by Kenneth J. Stein
www.filebox.vt.edu/forestry/wildlife/stein/insects.html

Complete Book List

Book Title	Author
Using children's literature to teach the scientific method	
Fortunately	by Remy Charlip
How to Think Like a Scientist: Answering Questions by the Scientific Method	by Stephen Kramer, illustrated by Felicia Bond
Suddenly	by Colin Mc Naughton
Magnets and testing hypotheses	
How to Think Like a Scientist: Answering Questions by the Scientific Method	by Stephen Kramer, illustrated by Felicia Bond
Marta's Magnets	by Wendy Pfeffer
What Makes a Magnet?	by Franklyn M. Branley

Year-round gardening

A Bear for All Seasons	by Diane Marcial Fuchs
Autumn	by Terri Degezelle
Chicken Soup with Rice: A Book of Months	by Maurice Sendak
My Mama Had a Dancing Heart	by Libba Moore Gray
Pieces: A Year in Poems & Quilts	by Anna Grossnickle Hines
When This Box Is Full	by Patricia Lillie
Winter: An Alphabet Acrostic	by Steven Schnur (author has written one book for each of the four seasons)
The Year at Maple Hill Farm	by Alice and Martin Provensen
Any book about the seasons	

Planting strawberry plants

Cook-A-Doodle-Doo!	by Janet Stevens and Susan Stevens Crummel
The First Strawberries, a Cherokee Story	by Joseph Bruchac
Garden	by Robert Maass
Good Job, Oliver!	by Laurel Molk
The Grey Lady and the Strawberry Snatcher	by Molly Bang
Jamberry	by Bruce Degen
The Little Mouse, the Red Ripe Strawberry and the Big Hungry Bear	by Don and Audrey Wood
Sweet Strawberries	by Phyllis Reynolds Naylor

What do seeds need to grow?

I'm a Seed	by Jean Marzollo
The Surprise Garden	by Zoe Hall

Why do some tree leaves change color?

Autumn Leaves	by Ken Robbins
How Leaves Change	by Sylvia A. Johnson
Red Leaf, Yellow Leaf	by Lois Ehlert
Trees, Leaves and Bark (Take-Along Guide)	by Diane L. Burns

Stretch your Senses—a walk to a nearby park

Autumn Leaves	by Ken Robbins
Good Mushrooms and Bad Toadstools	by Allan Fowler
I Wonder (Green Light Readers)	by Tana Hoban
A Log's Life	by Wendy Pfeffer
Looking Down	by Steve Jenkins
Meeting Trees	by Scott Russell Sanders
Red Leaf, Yellow Leaf	by Lois Ehlert
A Tree is Nice	by Janice May Udry

Crickets and using magnifiers

Broadsides From the Other Orders, A Book of Bugs	by Sue Hubbell
Compost Critters	by Bianca Lavies
It's a Good Thing There Are Insects	by Alan Fowler
"Leave That Cricket Be, Alan Lee"	by Barbara Ann Porte

More Pet Bugs	by Sally Kneidle
Pet Bugs	by Sally Kneidle
Squash It!	by Eric A. Kimmel
The Very Quiet Cricket	by Eric Carle

Compost critters

Compost Critters	by Bianca Lavies
Creepy Crawlies and the Scientific Method: More Than 100 Hands-On Science Experiments for Children	by Sally Kneidel
Pet Bugs: A Kid's Guide to Catching and Keeping Touchable Insects	by Sally Kneidel

Planting spring bulbs

Be Blest, a celebration of the seasons	by Mary Beth Owens
Planting a Rainbow	by Lois Elhert
Spring: An Alphabet Acrostic	by Steven Schnur
To Everything	by Bob Barner
When This Box is Full	by Patricia Lillie

Corn around the world, an introduction to the globe

Be Blest: A Celebration of the Seasons	by Mary Beth Owens
Corn is Maize: The Gift of the Indians	by Aliki
The Earth is Good, A Chant in Praise of Nature	by Michael DeMunn
Looking Down	by Steve Jenkins
Planet Earth/Inside Out	by Gail Gibbons

Winter birds

Any bird identification book	
Cardinal and Sunflowers	by James Preller
Counting Is for the Birds	by Frank Mazzola, Jr.
Crinkleroot's 25 Birds Every Child Should Know	by Jim Arnosky
Feathers for Lunch	by Lois Elhert
Have You Seen Birds	by Barbara Reid
Our Yard is Full of Birds	by Anne Rockwell
Snowballs	by Lois Elhert
Urban Roosts: Where Birds Nest in the City	by Barbara Bash

What is melting?

Once upon Ice: And Other Frozen Poems selected	by Jane Yolen
Solid, Liquid, or Gas?	by Fay Robinson

What can wind do?

Gilberto and the Wind	by Marie Hall Ets
Let's Try It Out in the Air: Hands-On Early-Learning Science Activities	by Seymour Simon and Nicole Fauteux

Planting peas on Presidents' day

Grandpa's Garden Lunch *	by Judith Caseley
Inch by Inch: The Garden Song	by David Mallett, et al
The Ugly Vegetables	by Grace Lin

Waiting for mantises to hatch

Backyard Hunter: The Praying Mantis	by Bianca Lavies
How to Hide a Butterfly and Other Insects	by Ruth Heller
Mealworms, Raise Them, Watch Them, See Them Change	by Adrienne Mason
Pet Bugs: A Kid's Guide to Catching and Keeping Touchable Insects	by Sally Kneidel
Creepy Crawlies and the Scientific Method: More Than 100 Hands-On Science Experiments for Children	by Sally Kneidel
Bugs! Bugs! Bugs!	by Bob Barner

A tree is nice

Are Trees Alive?	by Debbie S. Miller, illustrated by Stacey Schuett
Autumn Leaves	by Ken Robbins
I Am a Leaf	by Jean Marzollo
A Log's Life	by Wendy Pfeffer
Maples in the Mist	by Minfong Ho
Meeting Trees	by Scott Russell Sanders
Oak Tree	by Paul Fleisher
Old Elm Speaks: Tree Poems	by Kristine O'Connell George, illustrated by Kate Kiesler
A Tree Is Growing by Arthur Dorros *A Tree Is Nice*	by Janice May Udry

Dirt, what is it?

Compost Critters	by Bianca Lavies
The Piggy in the Puddle	by Charlotte Pomerantz and James Marshall

Butterflies change as they grow

Butterfly Gardens, Luring Nature's Loveliest Pollinators to Your Yard	edited by Alcinda Lewis
From Caterpillar to Butterfly	by Deborah Heiligman
How to Hide a Butterfly and Other Insects	by Ruth Heller
Mealworms, Raise Them, Watch Them, See Them Change	by Adrienne Mason,
Waiting for Wings	by Lois Ehlert
Where Butterflies Grow	by Joanne Ryder

Planting a butterfly garden

Butterflies in the Garden	by Carol Lerner
How to Hide a Butterfly and Other Insects	by Ruth Heller
Miss Hallberg's Butterfly Garden	by Gay Bishop, illustrated by Kathy Geotzel
The Surprise Garden	by Zoe Hall
Waiting for Wings	by Lois Ehlert
Where Butterflies Grow	by Joanne Ryder

What is it?

ABC Science Riddles	by Barbara Saffer, illustrated by Jennifer Johnson Haywood
How to Think Like a Scientist: Answering Questions by the Scientific Method	by Stephen Kramer

Look Book	by Tana Hoban
Mouse Views, What the Classroom Pet Saw	by Bruce McMIllan
Sense Suspense, a Guessing Game for the Five Senses	by Bruce McMIllan
When Riddles Come Rumbling: Poems to Ponder	by Rebecca Kai Dotlich, illustrated by Karen Dugan

Rocks that are made of little pieces (sedimentary)

The Pebble in My Pocket	by Meredith Hooper
Peterson First Guide to Rocks and Minerals	by Frederick H. Pough
Planet Earth/Inside Out	by Gail Gibbons
Rocks and Minerals	by Joel Arem
Simon and Schuster's Guide to Rocks and Minerals	by Martin Prinz, George Harlow, and Joseph Peters
Solid, Liquid, or Gas?	by Fay Robinson

Rocks that were melted (igneous) and volcanoes

Hill of Fire	by Thomas Lewis
Planet Earth/Inside Out	by Gail Gibbons
Solid, Liquid, or Gas?	by Fay Robinson

Not all fossils are dinosaurs

Footprints in the Snow	by Cynthia Benjamin
Fossils Tell of Long Ago	by Aliki

Mirrors reflect light

I see Me!	by Pegi Deitz Shea, illustrated by Lucia Washburn
Reflections	by Ann Jonas
Seven Sillies	by Joyce Dunbar
Shadows and Reflections	by Tana Hoban

Working with pumps, siphons, and capillary action

How Things Work	by Neil Ardley

Taking note of volume

Capacity	by Henry Pluckrose
Cook-A-Doodle-Doo!	by Janet Stevens and Susan Stevens Crummel
The Crow and the Pitcher (sometimes called *The Thirsty Crow*)	One of Aesop's Fables
Cubes, Cones, Cylinders and Spheres	by Tana Hoban
Solid, Liquid, or Gas?	by Fay Robinson

Evaporation and condensation

Down Comes the Rain	by Franklyn M. Branley

Sound is vibration

And the Cow Said Moo!	by Mildred Phillips, illustrated by Sonja Lamut

Listen to the Desert/Oye Al Desierto	by Pat Mora, illustrated by Francisco X. Mora
Marsh Music	by Marianne Collins Berkes, illustrated by Robert Noreika
Slop Goes the Soup: A Noisy Warthogs Word Book	by Pamela Duncan Edwards, illustrated by Henry Cole
Sounds All Around	by Wendy Pfieffer

Making a chemical reaction to create slime

Kids' Crazy Concoctions: 50 Mysterious Mixtures for Art and Craft Fun	by Jill Frankel Hauser
Mud Pies and Other Recipes: A Cookbook for Dolls	by Marjorie Winslow, illustrated by Erik Blegvad
Pancakes for Breakfast	by Tomie de Paola
Piggy in the Puddle	by Charlotte Pomerantz
Pretend Soup and Other Real Recipes: A Cookbook for Preschoolers and Up	by Mollie Katzen and Ann L. Henderson

Eating sunlight

Bread Is for Eating	by David and Phillis Gershator
Counting Cows	by Woody Jackson
Little Green Thumbs	by Mary An Van Hage, et al
The Milk Makers	by Gail Gibbons
Sun Bread	by Elisa Kleven
The Sun is My Favorite Star	by Frank Asch

Objects in motion

101 Science Poems & Songs For Young Learners (see poem "Gravity")	by Meish Goldish
Calder: 1898-1976 (Album Series)	by Jacob Baal-Teshuva and Alexander Calder
Isaac Newton and Gravity	by Steve Parker
The Science Book of Gravity	by Neil Ardley

Our sense of touch

Feely Bugs: To Touch and Feel	by David A. Carter
Looking Out for Sarah	by Glenna Lang
My Five Senses	by Aliki
Pat the Bunny	by Dorothy Kunhardt
Seven Blind Mice	by Ed Young
Touch (Explore Your Senses)	by Laurence P. Pringle

Mixing and separating colors

All the Colors We Are	by Katie Kissinger
The Colors of Us	by Karen Katz
Planting a Rainbow	by Lois Ehlert
Rainbow Joe and Me	by Maria Diaz Strom
Tell Me a Season	by Mary McKenna Siddals

Our sense of smell

Dog Breath! The horrible Trouble with Hally Tosis	by Dav Pilkey
My Five Senses	by Aliki
Smelling Things	by Alan Fowler
Two Eyes a Nose and a Mouth	by Roberta G. Intrater

Wheels are tools

Galimoto	by Karen Lynn Williams
How Willie Got His Wheels	by Deborahne Turner and Diana Mohler, illustrated by Rhonda McHugh
Load'Em Up Trucks (Mighty Wheels Series)	by Debora Pearson, illustrated by Chum McLeod
What Is Round?	by Rebecca Kai Dotlich
Wheels (Step Into Reading)	by Annie Cobb, illustrated by Davy Jones

Bubbles

Cubes, Cones, Cylinders and Spheres	by Tana Hoban
Is It Rough? Is It Smooth? Is It Shiny?	By Tana Hoban
The Nature and Science of Bubbles	by Jane Burton and Kim Taylor
Pop! : A Book About Bubbles (Let's-Read-And-Find-Out Science)	by Kimberly Brubaker Bradley, Margaret Miller (Photographer)

Recycling paper

Crashed, Smashed, and Mashed	by Joyce Slayton Mitchell
Each Living Thing	by Joanne Ryder, illustrated by Ashley Wolff
The Earth Is Good, A Chant in Praise of Nature	by Michael DeMunn
The Great Trash Bash	by Loren Leedy
Here Comes the Recycling Truck!	by Meyer Seltzer
Joseph Had a Little Overcoat	by Simms Taback
Pollution and Waste	by Rosie Harlow
Recycle That!	by Fay Robinson
Recycle!	by Gail Gibbons
This Is Our Earth	by Laura Lee Benson
You're Aboard Spaceship Earth	by Patricia Lauber

Rocket ships blasting off

BLAST OFF! A Space Counting Book	by Norma Cole
Cutaway Space Vehicles	by Jon Richards
I Want to Be an Astronaut	by Byron Barton
Space Exploration	by Carole Stott
The Space Shuttle	by Jaqueline Langille and Bobbie Kalman

Measuring hands

How Tall, How Short, How Faraway	by David A. Adler
Length	by Henry Pluckrose
Measuring Penny	by Loreen Leedy
Twelve Snails to One Lizard: A Tale of Mischief and Measurement	by Susan Hightower

Out-of-Print Book List

Note: These books are out of print, but are worth trying to find because they support the science activities very well.

Book Title   Author

Planting strawberry plants

Strawberry   by Jennifer Coldrey

What do seeds need to grow?

A Seed is a Promise   by Claire Merrill
All About Seeds   by Melvin Berger
Bean and Plant   by Christine Back and Barrie Watts
Grandpa's Garden Lunch   by Judith Caseley
How a Seed Grows   by Helene J. Jordan
Seeds   by George Shannon

Why do some tree leaves change color?

Fresh Fall Leaves   by Betsy Franco

Stretch your senses—a walk to a nearby park

Where is the Fly?   by Caron Lee Cohen

Crickets and using magnifiers

Look Closer   by Brian and Rebecca Wildsmith
Wetlands Nature Search   by Andrew Langley

Compost critters

It's A Good Thing There Are Insects   Allan Fowler

Planting spring bulbs

A Flower Grows   by Ken Robbins
A Year in the City   by Kathy Henderson
What Comes in Spring   by Barbara Horton

Corn around the world, an introduction to the globe

Half-a-Ball of Kenkiby   by Verna Aardema
People of Corn   by Mary-Joan Gerson
What Can She Be?   by Gloria and Esther Goldreich

Winter birds

A Year of Birds   by Ashley Wolff

What can wind do?

Bizzy Bones and Uncle Ezra   by Jacqueline Briggs Martin

Experiments With Air	by Ray Broekel
The Wind	by Jeanne Bendick
The Wind Blew	by Pat Hutchins

Planting peas on Presidents' day

All About Seeds	by Melvin Berger
Bean and Plant	by Christine Back and Barrie Watts
Grandpa's Garden Lunch	by Judith Caseley
How a Seed Grows	by Helene J. Jordan
A Seed is a Promise	by Claire Merrill
Seed	by George Shannon

Waiting for mantises to hatch

BUGS	by Nancy W. Parker and Joan R. Wright

A tree is nice

I Found a Leaf	by Sharon Lerner
Tree	by Althea
A Tree Is Nice	by Janice May Udry
Trees, a poem	by Harry Behn

Dirt, what is it?

Under the Ground a first discovery book	by G. Jeunesse and P. de Bourgoin

Rocks that are made of little pieces (sedimentary)

It Could Still Be a Rock	by Alan Fowler

Rocks that were melted (igneous) and volcanoes

It Could Still Be a Rock	by Alan Fowler

Not all fossils are dinosaurs

It Could Still Be a Rock	by Alan Fowler

Mirrors reflect light

The Magic Mirror Book	by Marion Walter

Working with pumps, siphons, and capillary action

The Science Book of Water	by Neil Ardley
Water and Floating	by David Evans and Claudette Williams

Evaporation and condensation

Puddles	by Jonathan London

Sound is vibration

Crash! Bang! Boom!	by John Spier
The Indoor Noisy Book	by Margaret Wise Brown
Max, the Music-maker	by Miriam B. Stecher and Alice S. Kandell
Rat-a-Tat, Pitter Pat	by Alan Benjamin and Margaret Miller
Shake, Rattle and Strum	by Sara Corbett

Making a chemical reaction to create slime

Muddigush   by Kimberley Knutson

Eating sunlight

Brown Cow Green Grass Yellow Mellow Sun   by Ellen Jackson
The Sun's Day   by Mordicai Gerstein

Objects in motion

The Ball Bounced   by Nancy Tafuri
Gravity is a Mystery   by Franklyn M. Branley
Wheel Away!   by Dayle Ann Dodds

Our sense of touch

Lucy's Picture   by Nicola Moon
Touching   by Henry Pluckrose

Mixing and separating colors

Little Blue and Little Yellow: A Story for Pippo and Other Children   by Leo Lionni

Wheels are tools

Wheels   by Byron Barton

Rocket ships blasting off

Astronauts Are Sleeping   by Natalie Standiford
Richie's Rocket   by Joan Anderson
Space Vehicles   by Anne Rockwell and David Brion

Measuring hands

Inch by Inch   by Leo Lionni

INDEX